"This is a concise, informative, and down-to-earth account of the people in the New Testament whose lives were touched by Jesus. For the general reader it opens new vistas in understanding the way people related to Jesus and how this relates to our situation today. Enriching."

Richard V. Pierard, scholar in residence, Gordon College

"Dr. Kistemaker writes engagingly and with sensitivity to the text of Scripture. He brings the characters of the Gospels to life in such a way that our own conversations with Jesus are enriched. Lay readers will find this book accessible, dependable, and spiritually enriching."

Gareth Lee Cockerill, professor of New Testament and biblical theology,
Wesley Biblical Seminary

"Simon J. Kistemaker, whose erudition and helpful publications in New Testament studies are well known, has tapped into that scholarship to produce a work whose prose, while simple enough for even a child to read, is grounded in a profound mastery of the Gospels materials. Here scholar and pastor meet, the one to dig deep into the life and ministry of Jesus as he encountered individual men and women, and the other to draw from those encounters lessons that are as pertinent and helpful to modern readers as they were to the original audiences."

Eugene Merrill, distinguished professor of Old Testament studies,
Dallas Theological Seminary

"The genius of this book is the conception itself—a survey and analysis of all the important conversations of Jesus recorded in the four Gospels. The result is an ever-expanding picture of Jesus and the people with whom he interacted. At the same time, as you keep reading this survey it will gradually dawn on you that the conversations of Jesus are a microcosm of the Gospels and their message."

Leland Ryken, Clyde S. Kilby Professor of English, Wheaton College

"Discerning readers will find in Kistemaker's thoughtful book not only useful background information to illumine Jesus' conversataions with forty-five individuals or groups but also helpful application for our lives today."

Ronald Youngblood, professor of Old Testament,
International College and Graduate School

"Simon Kistemaker has spent a lifetime as a New Testament scholar and commentator explaining and applying the Bible. He has helped countless ministers, students, and laypeople with his clear and straightforward expositions of Scripture. In these brief and inviting vignettes, with his usual combination of pithiness and helpfully suggestive applications, he shows us Jesus in conversation with very different kinds of people. These incidents, real historical encounters with Christ, come alive in Kistemaker's illuminations of texts from the Gospels and Acts. In reading this book, pastors and teachers alike will be helped in practically and devotionally applying God's truth, and the Christian public will be supplied with a faithful, heartwarming, elucidation of Jesus' ministry to all kinds of people."

J. Ligon Duncan III, pastor, First Presbyterian Church, Jackson, Mississippi

"With great insightfulness Dr. Kistemaker gives us the setting of and expounds to us Jesus' conversations. Those he conversed with are many and varied: those who became messengers, such as Nicodemus and the Samaritan woman, as well as those who opposed him, and a number of other groups in between. But on each Jesus' words left their mark. Take and read and let his conversations draw you in and also impact you."

George W. Knight III, adjunct professor of New Testament,
Greenville Presbyterian Theological Seminary

"Professor Kistemaker has done an excellent job in portraying a gentler side of Jesus in his dealings with people, and has done so with vivid language that makes each of the forty-six episodes both captivating and educational."

Robert L. Thomas, professor of New Testament, The Master's Seminary

"Every now and then a book comes out that makes one ask, why didn't I think of that? The Conversations of Jesus is long overdue, and Kistemaker has done a terrific job of showing how Jesus related to people and of providing a great model for our own ministries. It is lucid, readable, and informative. The organization is very helpful, and we see quickly how Jesus confronted and challenged the different individuals with whom he interacted. I especially appreciated how Jesus challenged his opponents—an area none of us handles very well."

Grant Osborne, professor of New Testament, Trinity Evangelical Divinity

THE
Conversations
OF JESUS

LEARNING FROM HIS ENCOUNTERS

SIMON J. KISTEMAKER

BakerBooks
Grand Rapids, Michigan

© 2004 by Simon J. Kistemaker

Published by Baker Books
a division of Baker Publishing Group
P.O. Box 6287, Grand Rapids, MI 49516-6287
www.bakerbooks.com

Printed in the United States of America

Library of Congress Cataloging-in-Publication Data
Kistemaker, Simon.
    The conversations of Jesus : learning from his encounters / Simon J.
Kistemaker.
        p.   cm.
    ISBN 0-8010-6490-2 (pbk.)
    1. Jesus Christ—Friends and associates. 2. Christian life. I. Title.
BS2430.K55 2004

232.9'5—dc22   2004005977

Scripture translations in this book are the author's own.

To
My dear wife, Jean
And
All our children and their spouses
And
All our grandchildren

Contents

Introduction

Jesus met all kinds of people. He dined with the rich, associated with the outcasts, had pity on those who lived in sin, and helped the poor and needy. He could be compared to an elevator that ascends from below ground level to the top of a high-rise building and descends again. At every level of society, Jesus spoke the right words at the right time.

He addressed people in such a manner that the simpleminded could understand his message and the learned had to ponder his statements. He immediately perceived that Pharisees, Sadducees, teachers of the law, and Herodians came to him with deceit, falsehood, trickery, intrigue, and plots to kill him. His compassion was genuine for those who had fallen into sin and needed his help; his love had no limits for those who sincerely sought him; and his patience with his disciples was seemingly endless. His heart went out to the multitudes milling around devoid of spiritual care like sheep without a shepherd. He ministered to them, and consequently the common people heard him gladly.

Jesus was such a great teacher that people came by the thousands from everywhere in Israel and beyond to listen to him. They were captivated by his words. The people understood his message because it was straightforward and profound. They came because the clergy of that day failed miserably to teach them the Word of God. By contrast, Jesus taught profound spiritual truths in a mode that the crowds could grasp and absorb as their daily food and drink. They refused to let him go and followed him wherever he went.

According to John's Gospel, Jesus does not utter the word *repent*. Instead, he engages the persons he meets in a dialogue that exposes their sins, shortcomings, and mistaken notions. When Jesus removes their masks, he speaks words of restoration instead of rebuke. He proves to be the gentle shepherd who finds the lost sheep and brings them back to the fold.

Jesus continues to attract countless followers throughout the world today. He draws the poverty-stricken masses in Africa, Asia, Central and South America, and in the slums of Western cities. He addresses the rich and tells them to sell all that they have and become his disciples. He fills us with faith, hope, and love. He invites all who are worn down by sin to come to him. He ushers us into a loving relationship with God, the giver of every good and perfect gift. And last, he wants us to take up our own crosses and follow him on the pathway that leads to peace and righteousness.

Jesus makes us members of his family and is not ashamed to call us his brothers and sisters. And we, being part of his household, are his joyful servants. We humbly walk in his footsteps and, in obedience to him, do his will.

People Who Became Messengers of Jesus

Πicodemus

JOHN 3, 7, AND 19

Under Cover of Darkness

Nicodemus was a Jew with a Greek name that means "conqueror of the people." Perhaps he was born somewhere in a country along the Mediterranean Sea where Greek was his native language. But in time he moved to Israel to be educated in the city of Jerusalem. He had an interest in the Scriptures and eventually became an interpreter of the Law of Moses. By joining the synagogue party of the Pharisees, he fulfilled his desire to be with those who had studied the sacred writings. In that party, he probably served as a scribe.

He climbed the social ladder and eventually attained the rank of councilor in the Jewish government, called the Sanhedrin. Because he understood the Scriptures, he had an influential voice in the leadership circles of Israel. In a sense, he lived up to his name: he was indeed a conqueror of the people.

One night while Jesus was in Jerusalem to celebrate the Passover Feast, Nicodemus went to meet him. He had heard Jesus speak and was impressed with the message he taught. This teacher not only read the Scriptures, he also explained and applied them like no one else in Israel. And Nicodemus had observed Jesus performing miracles of healing on those who were sick or handicapped.

So interested was Nicodemus in Jesus' teaching and healing ministry that he began to ask himself whether this man was the Messiah. He could honestly say that no one in Israel's history had ever performed the miracles that Jesus was doing.

But if Nicodemus were to be seen with Jesus in broad daylight, he would be criticized by his fellow councilmen. Thus he went to him at night, when he was free from official duties and could safely talk at length with the teacher from Nazareth.

A Heart-Changing Conversation

Nicodemus addressed Jesus as "rabbi," a respectful title that means "my great [teacher]." He was the older of the two by at least forty years, and as a councilor, he commanded great respect. But he addressed Jesus deferentially: "Rabbi, we know that you are a teacher who has come from God. For no one is able to do these miracles you do, unless God is with him."

Addressed as teacher, Jesus responded to Nicodemus true to his tutorial vocation. He introduced his teaching with words that expressed absolute certainty: "I can assure you of this truth." And what was that truth? "No one can see the kingdom of God unless he or she is born again." This was not the comment Nicodemus had expected to hear. Why didn't Jesus respond by saying he was pleased with Nicodemus' acknowledgment that Jesus' teaching and miracles demonstrated that God was with him? All that Nicodemus wanted was a confirmation that Jesus indeed was the promised Messiah.

But if Jesus had indicated he was pleased to hear that his work was appreciated, Nicodemus would have understood him only with his mind and not with his heart, which still throbbed in spiritual darkness. Hence Jesus taught him on two subjects of note: the kingdom of God and being born again.

The kingdom of God refers to God's administrative rule on earth. As a councilor in the Sanhedrin, Nicodemus certainly would have understood how government must enact and enforce laws to rule the nation of Israel. Yet he did not know how to apply spiritually God's rule in everyday life. To do this, he would need a heart that √ was conceived in heaven and born on earth. Jesus simply told Nicodemus, "You must be born anew; namely, your spiritual birth must come from heaven."

Nicodemus did not understand what Jesus meant by being born spiritually. He asked how an elderly person like himself could be born physically a second time. Jesus repeated his statement and then said, "Unless you are born of water and the Spirit, you cannot enter the kingdom of God."

Jesus hinted at a passage in the prophecy of Ezekiel (36:25–26) that Nicodemus, as a student of the Old Testament, should have known. God had said to the people of Israel, "I will sprinkle clean water on you, and you will be clean; I will cleanse you from all impurities and from your idols. I will give you a new heart and put a new spirit in you; I will remove from you your heart of stone and give you a heart of flesh." God said he would sprinkle clean water on his people and fill them with a new spirit so that they might be his holy people.

Nicodemus knew that the priests and Levites at the temple had to wash their hands and feet before entering the temple. He also knew that to serve God in that holy place and to function effectively with a new spirit in the religious life of Israel, the spiritual leaders needed a new heart.

Certainties Touching the Heart

Jesus taught Nicodemus spiritual truths so his student could see the difference between material and spiritual matters. A human body gives birth to a human body, but the Holy Spirit gives birth to a new spirit. This means that a change in a human spirit takes place only through the working of God's Spirit. Whenever the Holy Spirit touches a person's heart, his or her life changes radically for the better.

There is something mysterious about the coming and going of the Spirit. Jesus compared it to the blowing of the wind. No human controls the wind; it changes direction at will, increases in force, or tempers its effect in short order. Jesus told Nicodemus, "So it is with everyone born of the Spirit."

This is a mystery to people who have not been born anew and consequently have difficulty understanding what motivates those whose heart the Holy Spirit has renewed. Nicodemus was one of them and asked Jesus how this could be. With a chuckle in his voice, Jesus asked, "Are you a teacher in Israel and you do not know these things?"

There are two spheres in this universe; the one is physical, the other spiritual. Some people understand only the physical because they lack spiritual discernment; others have been blessed spiritually and know that the Spirit of God has given them rebirth. Some see only with their physical eyes while others, enlightened by the Spirit, see heavenly things. The one has been born physically while the other has experienced both a physical and a spiritual birth.

There is a profound difference between earthly and heavenly things. Jesus told Nicodemus, "If I have told you earthly things and you do not believe, how will you believe when I tell you heavenly things?" Jesus came to teach God's truth and to die on a cross. And people who understand this truth demonstrate faith in him and are recipients of eternal life.

The message Jesus taught Nicodemus was that he would believe with all his heart the words he himself had uttered to Jesus: "We know that you are a teacher who has come from God." Jesus brought the gospel to a political leader in Israel who, when converted, would be a spokesman for the Lord to defend and promote his cause.

A Councilor's Commitment

The name of Nicodemus appears in John's gospel on two successive occasions: at the Jewish Feast of Tabernacles and at the Feast of Passover (John 7 and 19, respectively). First, in mid-October, half a year before Jesus' death, Jesus preached publicly in the temple courts during the Feast of Tabernacles. The chief priests and the Pharisees sent temple guards to arrest him, but these guards were so enthralled by Jesus' teachings that they returned empty-handed.

Intrigued by Jesus' words, many believed and urged him to lodge with them, which he did. Jesus stayed two days and still more people in this Samaritan town put their faith in him. Furthermore, although they were convinced initially by the woman's evangelistic efforts, they now told her that her testimony was no longer needed. They now heard for themselves and were convinced that Jesus was the Savior of the world. Indeed, the Messiah in person and work was not bound to the nation of the Jews but was reaching out to the entire world.

An uneducated, immoral, and rejected Samaritan woman was converted and became an evangelist for Jesus Christ. She persuaded her fellow countrymen to put their faith in him. Jesus sent her into the harvest, in accordance with his Word: "The harvest is bountiful but the workers are few."

Application

Hidden sin makes us ill at ease, to say the least. But when a wise counselor talks to us in private and takes the covers off, we experience an overwhelming sense of relief. We admit that sin blinds us until our cover is removed. Then we see clearly again and are able to rectify our lives. No matter how deep we have fallen and how far we have gone astray, Jesus will release us from the burdens of sin and guilt to make us his servants.

Forgiven sinners express their thanks and joyously point others to Jesus. But many of us come to church on Sundays and miss this joyous sense of forgiveness. Indeed, a person can be in a sacred place of worship and still be far removed from God. We must ask Jesus to open our spiritual eyes, and we must seek forgiveness of sin. Then, in a hiding place alone with God, we feel his sacred presence. The Father actively seeks the person who comes to him in a spirit of true worship. As a God of love and light, he meets his people through his Son, Jesus Christ.

LEGI⊙N

A Man with Demons

A relative of mine was a schizophrenic. One moment he was a warm, kind, and considerate person; the next, his flashing anger consumed him. He was then a totally different person—even dangerous to the members of his family. I can't help but think of him when reading in Scripture about the demon-possessed man who lived on the east side of the Lake of Galilee in a town that today is known as Kursi.

This man was a member of the Gerasene people. At one time, he had been a respectful citizen and an asset to the community. Then a multitude of demons took up residence in this hapless person, so that he became a danger to his fellow citizens. For them his presence was a continual annoyance and a great embarrassment.

The man constantly shouted at the top of his voice and walked naked through the town. The townspeople tried to subdue him, but the demons gave him superhuman strength. He broke ropes, cords, fetters, and even leg irons; no one was able to restrain him.

26

Having no other place to keep him, they had left him among the caves where they buried the dead. He would come out of these caves and roam about in the open.

Jesus and his disciples had crossed the Lake of Galilee and moored on its east side. They now entered Gentile territory. They had not gone too far when they saw a large herd of pigs feeding in the lush grass of a hillside near a burial area. Suddenly they noticed a wild man who was unclothed and demon-possessed rushing toward them. No doubt the disciples asked themselves why Jesus wanted to expose them to physical harm. They wondered whether he would overpower this violent man.

When Jesus asked the man to identify himself, a demon spoke up. "Legion is my name, for we are many." A Roman legion consisted of six thousand men, but in colloquial speech, the word *legion* had taken on the general meaning of numerous. As a consequence of being possessed by numerous demons, the Gerasene man had enormous strength, and no one on earth was able to control him. He was also the most powerful demon-possessed person that Jesus had met thus far in his ministry.

The people had taken the demoniac to this solitary place and secretly hoped that he would soon kill himself and be given a place in one of the tombs carved out of the cliffs. Here the man would often cut himself with sharp stones and walk around naked, which accentuated his gruesome appearance. His bloodcurdling shrieks were so fierce that everyone was deathly afraid to be near him. All the time his shrieks could be heard far and near as he moved among the caves and in the hills. The people did not know what to do with him and were at their wits' end.

When the demoniac saw Jesus leaving the boat and setting foot on land, he ran toward him. But instead of attacking Jesus, he fell on his knees and worshiped him. The demons in the man immediately recognized Jesus and realized his power over them. One demon, as their spokesman, yelled at the top of the man's voice, "What do you have to do with me, Jesus, Son of the Most High God?"

He knew that even with all their combined physical and spiritual strength, the demons could never defeat Jesus. They could have made the man run far away from Jesus, but like moths attracted to the light, these demons were irresistibly drawn to Jesus and had to acknowledge his divine authority.

The Demons' Dismal Fate

The demon acknowledged that Jesus possessed divine power. By swearing an oath, he appealed to God and in a loud voice cried out, "I swear to God, don't torture me." He knew very well that the Lord had the authority to send him and his fellow demons directly to hell.

Though the demoniac understood the fearsome power the numerous demons possessed, he sensed that in the presence of the Son of God, they were helpless. For Jesus compelled the demon to state his name and to add the explanation that "we are many." Jesus' purpose was to heal the man by setting him free from demonic oppression. He came to make him whole again by casting out of his body its many unwanted occupants. His first task was to restore the man, and his second was to dispatch the evil spirits.

The demons feared that Jesus would consign them to hell to be imprisoned in gloomy dungeons until the Judgment Day. Hence they implored Jesus not to send them out of the area but to allow them to enter the nearby herd of two thousand pigs. Jesus allowed them to do so, and the possessed herd rushed down the steep bank into the Lake of Galilee and drowned.

While the demons resided in the man, they tried to destroy him but were unable. Yet when they entered the pigs, they caused immediate and utter destruction of life. Jesus listened to their request and was fully aware that the time they spent in the pigs would be short. He assigned them to be in the water rather than in the wilderness and among the caves. Demons were thought to reside in arid places and uninhabited regions but not in water. To be dispatched to the waves of the Lake of Galilee was indeed punishment for them.

Why would Jesus allow the seemingly unjustifiable destruction of at least two thousand pigs, a huge loss to their owners? The destruction devastated a significant number of people in that area and severely disrupted the local economy.

The Jews were told not to own or consume pigs; according to the Law of Moses, these animals were unclean. By contrast Gentile owners kept them and made their living by feeding, selling, and slaughtering them. Certainly Jesus was not intending to make Jews out of Gentiles. What then was Jesus' reason for allowing the demons to do their destructive work and for impoverishing the local population? The answer is fourfold:

1. to rescue a human being from Satan's tyranny,
2. to show the pigs' owners the value of a human being,
3. to send the healed man back to his own people, and
4. to introduce the Gentiles to Jesus' Good News.

After the pigs had drowned, their herders rushed into town and countryside to bring the owners the devastating news. When the townspeople met Jesus and saw the demoniac clothed and in his right mind, they became afraid. They should have been grateful to Jesus for casting out the evil spirits and for restoring to them a fellow citizen. But when they considered the loss of their possessions, they asked Jesus to leave their region. They clearly preferred material riches to human beings. Because of their misplaced values, these people were in Satan's grip and needed to be set free.

Jesus agreed to their request and with his disciples made his way to the boat. When he was ready to go aboard, the man who had been demon-possessed asked permission to accompany him. But Jesus refused to take him along. He had healed the man for a purpose, namely, to go back to his own people as an evangelist and tell them about the wonders that God had performed in him.

The man returned home and became a missionary to his fellow citizens. He told them that Jesus was the Son of God, who came to save the people from the tyranny of the devil. Indeed, he was the best kind of missionary Jesus could ever have sent to the Gentile population of the Gerasenes.

- First, he fully understood the power that Satan wields over his subjects.

- Next, he could testify to the destruction that the devil had inflicted on him and on the pigs.

- Third, although the citizens had asked Jesus in ignorance to leave their shores, the man who had suffered much from the demons could tell them about Jesus' love and his desire to free all people from the clutches of Satan.

- And last, this man became a missionary, not as a Jew but as a Gentile who was fully at home among his fellow citizens and was now useful to the Lord.

Application

The fury of the Antichrist in today's world is equally as fearsome as that of the demonic forces during Jesus' ministry. Satan knows that his time on this earth is short. He sends forth his evil angels to destroy human lives, distort the truth, and dominate the world. Nonetheless, the gospel message penetrates every country and is unstoppable. Satan does not exercise supreme authority. Instead, Christ Jesus is King of Kings and Lord of Lords. Scripture teaches us that Jesus is the victor in the spiritual battle against Satan and that we with the Lord are, and will be, victorious.

John the Baptist

Promising Beginnings

The gospel writers identify John the Baptist, or John the Baptizer, as a messenger called by God. His message to the people was to repent and be baptized. He was a genuine prophet whom God sent to Israel some five hundred years after Malachi, the last prophet in the Old Testament era, had prophesied about him.

Malachi had prophesied that after him would come a herald who would prepare the way before the Lord. This herald would come dressed like the prophet Elijah, fearlessly proclaiming the Word of God. John indeed had appeared in the spirit and power of Elijah to prepare the people for the coming of the Messiah. He served Jesus as forerunner, to prepare the way before him.

John was born into a priestly family. His mother, Elizabeth, was a direct descendant of the high priest Aaron, and his father, Zechariah, was a priest who served in the temple of Jerusalem. John grew up in the hill country of Judea, probably to the south of Jerusalem. He was thoroughly familiar with the desert area to the south and east of the capital city and with the region of the lower Jordan Valley.

John was born about half a year before Jesus, and John was related to him through his mother, Elizabeth. John's parents were well along in age when he was born; they probably died when he was in his teenage years, and thus he received spiritual guidance from others. When he was about thirty years of age, he began his ministry.

Called to Preach and Baptize

John was the voice in the wilderness that called the people back to God. He told the clergy of that day to show sincerity in their repentance. He advised the crowds that came to hear him to share their possessions with the poor, and he admonished the tax collectors to be honest in their work by collecting only what was due. He instructed soldiers not to extort money from the people, not to accuse them falsely but to be content with their pay. He even rebuked Herod Antipas, who had married Herodias, the wife of his half brother Philip. For this rebuke John was apprehended and imprisoned.

John preached the message that the kingdom of heaven was near, and he revealed himself as a prophet of God. Because of his preaching, the people were drawn to this strange man, who, like Elijah, walked around in clothes made from camel's hair and wore a leather belt around his waist. This desert dweller, who lived alone and ate food that included grasshoppers and wild honey, exhibited all the characteristics of the prophet Elijah.

He showed the people that he rejected a life of ease and luxury, and he urged them to look for a person who was more powerful and worthy than he was. John pointed the crowd to Jesus, the Messiah, who was just then coming onto the scene to take John's place. In the prophet's own words, John had to decrease in influence and Jesus had to increase.

When John was preaching the message of repentance and inviting the people to be baptized in the Jordan River, messengers sent by the religious authorities in Jerusalem asked him if he was the Messiah. He answered no. Then they inquired whether he was the prophet Elijah. Again he said no. Then they wanted to know if he could be the Prophet whom Moses had predicted to be the

Messiah, and John once more denied it. And when they prompted him to divulge his identity, he revealed that he was the voice in the desert appointed by God to prepare the way for the Lord. He was the messenger whom God had sent to make everything ready for the Messiah.

Some of the religious leaders, called Pharisees, were not satisfied with John's answers and demanded to know why he was baptizing people if he was not the Christ, Elijah, or the Prophet. Then John told them that there was a fundamental difference between him and the Messiah. He said that he baptized with water but that the Christ would come to baptize them with the Holy Spirit and with fire.

Comparing himself with the Christ, John said, "I am not even worthy to untie the laces of his sandals." He added that Jesus, who came after him, surpassed him because Jesus was before him. This appears contradictory, for how could Jesus come after John and yet emerge earlier on the scene? An older person deserves respect from one who is younger. Thus John should receive greater honor. But John deferred to Jesus and honored him who is the eternal Christ. Jesus could say to the religious leaders, "Before Abraham was born, I am" (John 8:58).

Baptizing the Sinless One

John met Jesus face-to-face at the Jordan River when he was baptizing people who repented of their sins. His act was different from the ritual washings performed by the Qumran community, because his was administered only once and symbolized the forgiveness of sins. John baptized the people who turned away from a sinful life, committed themselves to serving God, and looked forward to the coming of the Messiah.

When Jesus came to John and asked him to be baptized, John was perplexed. He objected to this request, saying that instead Jesus should baptize him. Why would the sinless Messiah need to be baptized? But Jesus told him that he should permit this baptism to fulfill all righteousness. Jesus' statement needs a word of explanation. What he indicated was that

- he had come on the scene as the Messiah,
- he had fully identified himself with those he had come to save,
- he was the sin-bearer of his people, and
- he was ready to begin his ministry.

In short, Jesus had to be made like his people in every way so that he effectively could minister to them.

John was the forerunner, and at the Jordan River it was his task to point the people to Jesus. He saw Jesus approaching him and said, "Look, the Lamb of God that takes away the sin of the world!" He looked to the end of Jesus' life, for on the cross, Jesus was the sacrificial Lamb that was slain just before the Jewish Passover Feast.

The following day, when two of John's disciples were with him, he saw Jesus again and said, "Look, the Lamb of God!" He then directed these disciples to follow Jesus so that they might switch their allegiance and become disciples of the Lord. We assume that one was John, the son of Zebedee; we know that the other was Andrew, the brother of Simon Peter. Jesus invited John and Andrew to stay with him for the greater part of a day and learn from him that he indeed is the Messiah, the Christ.

A Prisoner's Doubt and Assurance

John had been imprisoned on the east side of the Dead Sea because he had rebuked Herod Antipas for marrying Herodias, the wife of his half brother Philip. While in prison, John heard about the work and conduct of Jesus, who entered the homes of rich Pharisees and had dinner with them. Also, Jesus associated with social and moral outcasts in Israel, namely, tax collectors and prostitutes.

Although Jesus had begun his ministry with the message of repentance and the nearness of the kingdom of heaven, in time his message changed to parables and discourses. In addition, instead of wearing the same garb as the Baptist, Jesus was dressed in an expensive seamless garment that was woven in one piece from top to bottom.

Because of these things, doubt entered John's mind, and when his disciples came to him in his prison cell, he would discuss with them that Jesus' lifestyle differed from his own. He would question whether Jesus was indeed the Messiah. Finally, he sent two of his disciples to him to ask, "Are you the one who was to come or do we expect someone else?"

John was disappointed in Jesus, who was not cut from the same cloth as he was. John needed reassurance from Jesus, who conducted a curative ministry. It was a ministry of giving sight to the blind, healing the sick, restoring the lepers, making the deaf to hear and the lame to walk, casting out demons, raising the dead, and preaching the gospel to the poor.

From the Old Testament, John should have known that only the Messiah could perform this miraculous ministry. Jesus proved by word and deed that he was indeed the Christ sent by God the Father. And John should have been reassured that his task as forerunner had not been in vain. The kingdom of heaven had undeniably arrived, as Jesus' ministry proved.

Jesus spoke well of John the Baptist and gave him the highest honor a person could receive. He called him a prophet whose place in life had not been surpassed by any human being. He said that John was the prophet who appeared as Elijah of old and was sent to prepare the people for the messianic age. John's life came to a sudden end in prison, where he was beheaded.

John's Continued Legacy

Three days before Jesus' death, he was teaching at the temple in Jerusalem. The chief priests, the teachers of the law, and the elders came to him and asked by what authority he was teaching. Instead of answering directly, Jesus asked them a question. If they answered him, he would reply to their inquiry.

Jesus asked whether John's baptism was from God or from men. When John began his ministry at the Jordan, these leaders had sent priests and Levites to John with the same question.

Now confronting Jesus, they had to answer his question concerning John's authority. If they should reply, "John's authority came from God," Jesus would ask them, "Why did you not believe in

him?" And should they say, "From men," they would discredit John
in the eyes of the public, who considered him to be a prophet.
They refused to answer him. This gave Jesus the freedom to say
that he would not tell them by what authority he was teaching and
performing miracles.

John's influence as a prophet did not cease at the moment of his
death. Some twenty-five years later in Ephesus, nearly a thousand
miles from Judea, Paul met twelve disciples of John the Baptist. He
baptized them in the name of Jesus, and they received the Holy
Spirit and preached in different languages (Acts 19:1–7). They
spread the name of Jesus wherever they went with his gospel.

Application

John's prophetic ministry lasted only half a year and then came
to an abrupt end in a dungeon. He accomplished what God had
planned for him, namely, to prepare the people for the coming of
the Messiah. His life demonstrates the reality of God's effective plan,
in which human beings take an active part. John's rule of life with
regard to Jesus was, "He must increase and I must decrease."

The sudden death of a person in the midst of his or her career
baffles us, and we ask the inevitable question, Why? God does not
give us a direct answer, but he does make it known that he determines
the length of our time on earth. When our task is completed in God's
eyes, he calls us home. But while we are on earth, he wants us to keep
our eyes fixed on Jesus, the captain and perfecter of our faith.

PEOPLE WHOSE FAITH JESUS PRAISED

The Centurion in Capernaum

MATTHEW 8 AND LUKE 7

An Officer in the Roman Army

The man was a centurion in the Roman army, probably in the service of Herod Antipas, who was appointed by Rome to rule Galilee. He was stationed in Capernaum along the northwest shore of the Lake of Galilee. The term *centurion* implies that he was a captain of one hundred soldiers. Most likely he was a Roman citizen who had befriended the Jewish population by attending worship services in the synagogue. He was a religious and God-fearing person who prayed to God and gave alms to the poor. He had a genuine affection for the Jewish people. When the congregation needed a new edifice, the centurion built a synagogue for them using his own resources. The Jews in Capernaum honored him for worshiping in the synagogue he had erected.

Jesus had performed numerous healing miracles in Capernaum. A demon-possessed man had entered the synagogue while Jesus was preaching and had disturbed the service with his loud cries. The

39

demon, speaking through the man, had shouted, "Ah, what have you to do with us, Jesus of Nazareth? Have you come to destroy us? I know who you are, the Holy One of God." Jesus had told the demon to come out of the man and be silent. The evil spirit had obeyed, to the utter amazement of all the people, for now they knew Jesus' identity. If the centurion had been present, he would have taken note of the demon's cry that Jesus was the Holy One of God.

On a certain day, a youthful servant of the centurion became ill with paralysis and was near death. He was dear to the centurion, who immediately thought of Jesus and sent Jewish representatives to him. These representatives were ruling elders in the town and in the synagogue. In the centurion's mind, it would be more suitable if they were to ask Jesus for help than if he did. They approached Jesus and asked him to come without delay to heal the boy.

A Gentile's Astounding Faith

Even though a Gentile might attend the worship services in the synagogue, a Jew might never enter the home of a Gentile, for he had to guard himself from being defiled. Similarly, a Gentile might not set foot in the home of a Jew. Between the Jew and the foreigner existed a wall of separation. For this reason, the centurion had asked the Jewish elders to approach Jesus on his behalf. If the elders agreed to be intermediaries, he thought, Jesus would not be offended. No one asked whether the boy could be carried to Jesus. The situation was urgent, and thus the call went out to Jesus to come immediately and heal the young man.

The elders were not merely messengers for the centurion; they also spoke to Jesus about the centurion's good name. They implored him to come without delay. They informed him that this man deserved help for two reasons: he loved the Jewish people, and he built their synagogue. Without a doubt Jesus knew all of this, for as a resident and a worshiper in Capernaum, he had become acquainted with this benevolent centurion.

The elders' plea was based on the centurion's worthiness. Did the Jews think that because of the official's generosity and friendliness he deserved to be heard? They adopted an attitude of returning a favor, but not so Jesus. At a later occasion, Jesus taught his followers the principle that after all the work they had done for him, they should consider themselves unworthy servants who only did their duty.

Without any objection, Jesus agreed to the request of the elders and accompanied them to the centurion's house. Even though the Jews had told Jesus that the centurion deserved to be helped, the man did not deem himself worthy to have Jesus come under his roof. He knew that Jesus had a power far greater than any human's. He saw his own position as a military officer as but a faint reflection of Jesus' greatness. So as Jesus was nearing the house, the centurion sent his friends with the message that he should not take the trouble to enter his house. This could be interpreted as a gesture intended to save a Jew the embarrassment of refusing to enter a Gentile home. But this was not the case. In the message relayed by his friends, the centurion used the title *Lord* to express his respect for Jesus' holiness. The centurion explained that he felt he was not worthy to be in the presence of Jesus' majesty.

As a military officer, the centurion was under the authority of his superiors, whose orders he had to carry out without question or delay. Similarly, he himself held the power to direct the soldiers under his command. He reasoned that if he as a centurion could expect immediate compliance, how much more would Jesus, with his immense power, be obeyed? He had faith that Jesus could heal the sick man merely by speaking the word. Jesus did not have to touch or even see him. Accordingly, he told Jesus to speak the word and order the sickness to leave the servant's body.

When Jesus heard these words coming from the lips of a Gentile, he was astounded by the man's faith. The Jewish population in Capernaum had observed all the miracles Jesus performed but failed to believe, yet this centurion acted in faith. Even though the unbelieving crowds in Capernaum had heard Jesus teach, they refused to repent. These were the people who were instructed in the Scriptures, who should have recognized Jesus as the Messiah promised by the prophets. Yet it was a Gentile drawn by the biblical teachings in the synagogue who acknowledged Jesus as the Holy One of God.

Jesus did not praise the Jews in Capernaum, who were highly privileged to have him dwell in their midst, but the Roman centurion, who put his faith in him. It is true that some Jewish people had expressed this faith. Nathanael had acknowledged him as the Messiah when he said, "Rabbi, you are the Son of God; you are the King of Israel." Even Peter uttered similar words: "You are the Christ, the Son of the living God." But these were his disciples, who received daily instruction. The centurion did not have that opportunity, yet he was the one who showed an understanding of spiritual truths. For him, Jesus was the Holy One of God.

After they had relayed their message, the elders and the friends of the centurion returned to the centurion's house to see what had happened. They found the youthful servant in robust health and strength. The lesson they learned was that Jesus always responds to people's faith. He rewards those who earnestly seek, trust, and love him. And when Jesus performs a miracle, it is to increase their faith.

Application

Jesus came to earth in human form and thus became one of us, though without sin. Because of this close relationship to us, people often forget that he is the Son of God, the Holy One, that he demands our highest respect.

If we ask anything in faith and in Jesus' name, he listens and acts on our requests. He has given us this promise: "If you ask me anything in my name, I will do it."

We should remember that God is never indebted to us when we show our love to him and to our neighbor. We cannot claim any reward or merit for performing a good deed. Instead, we humbly confess that all our deeds are incomplete and imperfect in his sight. His blessings, then, are not in response to our good works but stem from his grace and goodness to us in Christ Jesus.

A Syro-Phoenician Woman

MATTHEW 15 AND MARK 7

A Gentile Woman of Faith

She lived near Tyre, a seaport along the Mediterranean coast. She was not born there but had moved from Syrian Phoenicia, an area that now borders modern Syria and Lebanon. Before that time, she had come from Greece. She had heard about Jesus, for in this city he was the talk of the town because of the miracles he had performed in Israel and Galilee, and also because, teaching in Galilee, he had denounced the towns of Bethsaida, Capernaum, and Chorazin for their lack of faith in him. He had said that if the miracles he had performed in these places had been performed in Tyre and Sidon, they would have repented long ago in sackcloth and ashes.

All the people who were ill or afflicted by demonic spirits longed to see Jesus and to ask him to heal them.

Many people from the coastal cities of Tyre and Sidon had walked to Galilee to hear Jesus' message. But not everyone was able to travel to the land of Israel. Now Jesus had decided to come to Tyre. He wanted to be alone with his disciples away from all the opposition he had to endure in Galilee.

When Jesus arrived in Tyre, he entered a house and asked the owner for privacy, urging him to keep his presence a secret. But this secret proved to be impossible to keep. As Jesus and his twelve disciples entered the city, he was recognized. The news spread like wildfire through the city.

No sooner had Jesus arrived in Tyre than the Syro-Phoenician woman came to him, probably speaking Greek. She had recognized him, and in a loud voice, she called out addressing him as Lord, Son of David. This title was commonly used by Jewish people to identify the promised Messiah, yet it was also known among the Gentiles. The woman addressed him politely and reverently as both Lord and Messiah, showing her faith in Jesus as the Anointed One of God.

The woman's request was urgent. Her daughter, who was possessed by a demon, suffered relentless mental torture. The woman was distressed because of her inability to heal her daughter and because no one else could assist her.

When she saw Jesus, she knew that aid was near. Again and again she cried out to him, but he acted as if she did not exist. Eventually her repeated calls annoyed his disciples, who asked Jesus to send her away. For them, she was merely a woman and a Gentile. She was not worthy to be heard.

With her crying, she created an intolerable distraction. Jesus' disciples wanted to shield him from the embarrassment she caused. But Jesus adopted a different approach. He wanted to test the woman's faith and at the same time teach the disciples that faith is found not only among the Jews but also among the Gentiles.

Persistence Pays Off

Jesus responded to the woman's continued outcry by telling her that he was sent only to those who were lost and belonged to the nation of Israel. It was his indirect way of asking her why he should accede to her request. Kneeling before him, she kept imploring him to show her mercy: "Lord, help me!"

The seemingly harsh treatment she received was for her benefit and also was a lesson for the disciples. Jesus wanted them to observe this woman's faith. He told her that it would not be right to take the bread meant for the children and throw it to their pet dogs. Children have rights and privileges in the family, but not dogs. Although pet dogs ought to be fed, they are never placed on the level of children.

Once more the woman replied, now convincingly and to the point. She said, "Yes, Lord, but even the pet dogs eat the crumbs that fall from their master's table." Three times she addressed Jesus as Lord. And the third time she used Jesus' own words by reminding him that even pet dogs consume the same food as the children.

Jesus commended the woman for her great faith and granted her request. Her persistence received a favorable reply from Jesus. He had told his disciples that if they had faith like a mustard seed, the smallest of garden seeds, they would be able to move mountains. But she was a Gentile who did not grow up learning the Scriptures in a synagogue like the Jewish people did. Her knowledge of Jesus was hearsay, and yet she firmly believed that Jesus was Lord, the Son of David, the Messiah.

Merely by speaking the word, Jesus healed her daughter, for the demon left her that very moment. When the woman returned home, she found her daughter lying on the bed healed and of a sane mind. What joy and thankfulness there was in that home! She could tell her daughter what Jesus had done for her, even though he had not even entered their humble abode. Her daughter's restoration became the news of the day in Tyre. Consequently, the name and message of Jesus were spread throughout the land.

Why did Jesus prolong the woman's anxiety by not answering her promptly? We could say that Jesus wanted to test her faith, and that is correct. But it does not tell the whole story. Again we could say that Jesus wanted his disciples to learn a lesson in faith exemplified not by a son or daughter of Abraham but by a Gentile woman. That is correct too, but again it falls short of the mark.

The answer must be found in Jesus' teachings, namely, to persist in prayer and not give up. He repeatedly taught that believers should always go to God in prayer. He assured them that God hears his people who in prayerful expectation wait until he honors their petitions.

During his ministry on earth, Jesus often kept people waiting. Jairus had to wait for Jesus to heal his daughter, who was near death. And because of Jesus' being delayed along the way, he came too late, for the child had died. But Jesus demonstrated his power to raise her from the dead. Also, Mary and Martha, having sent an urgent message to Jesus about the severe illness of their brother, Lazarus, experienced the Lord's failure to come and heal their brother. Lazarus died and the sisters were cast into grief and sorrow. But once again Jesus brought the dead back to life to show God's glory.

These cases prove that the Lord tests the faith and endurance of those who petition him, so that his power and his glory may become evident in their lives. Similarly, Jesus wanted to test the Syro-Phoenician woman in the city of Tyre. Without a doubt she proved to be a woman who put great faith into action.

Application

In his first epistle, John writes that if we ask God anything that is in accordance with his will, he grants our request. He notes that God already has set it aside for us. We pray the petition, "Give us today *our* daily bread." We ask for food and claim it because the bread already belongs to us as we ask God to give it now, today.

Why does God seemingly turn a deaf ear to requests that we ask in faith and to the glory of his name? We learn from experience that he answers at his appointed time. God wants to test our faith so that we rely on him in complete confidence and know he will hear us.

A ROYAL OFFICIAL

JOHN 4

Faith in Action

He was a royal official serving Herod Antipas, the ruler of Galilee, whom the people generally called their king. This official most likely was a Jew and not a Gentile, and he lived in Capernaum. He had come to the town of Cana, the place where at a wedding Jesus had turned water into wine, to meet Jesus.

The reason this royal executive traveled to Cana was that his son was seriously ill. The official was aware of Jesus' healing powers. The people in Capernaum could testify to the numerous miracles Jesus had performed, including healing the sick, casting out demons, restoring sight to the blind, causing the paralytic to get up and walk, and raising the dead. When the official heard that Jesus had left Judea and come to Galilee, he traveled seven hours on foot to Cana and begged the Lord to come and heal his son, who was at death's door.

But Jesus responded to the royal official's request in much the same way he had to the woman in Tyre. He gave him a discouraging reply: "You people [the Jewish official and fellow countrymen]

have to see miraculous signs and wonders before you will ever
believe!" Jesus wanted the man to put his faith not in the miracle
of healing but in Jesus' divinity.

The woman of Syrian Phoenicia had responded to Jesus by addressing him as Lord, Son of David, to identify his divinity. But
the royal official uttered no such theological terms to gain Jesus'
consent for healing his son. He politely addressed Jesus as sir and
then implored him to come down before his little child passed away.
He indicated that time was of the essence and placed the urgency
of this case before Jesus. In a sense, he held Jesus responsible. The
thought that Jesus could raise his son from the dead did not even
enter his mind. He saw only the need of the hour.

Jesus granted the official's request and said, "Go home, your son
will live." With this command, Jesus wished to test the man's faith
and see whether he would depart. And so it happened, for the father
took Jesus at his word and believed that he had healed his son merely
by speaking the word. He immediately returned to Capernaum.

Because it was late, the official had to spend the night at a roadside
inn and continue his journey the following day. He had to travel
downhill from the heights of hilly Cana to the low point of nearly
seven hundred feet below sea level at Capernaum, which was situated
on the shores of the Lake of Galilee. Traveling on foot at the rate
of three miles per hour, the father returned to Capernaum perhaps
around noon the following day. When he approached Capernaum,
his servants came out to meet him with the news that his son was
alive and well. The news was so exhilarating that they had left the
house and met him on the road.

Exuberant Joy

The official sought to verify the exact hour when the miracle
of healing had occurred. The servants told him that the fever had
disappeared at seven o'clock the preceding evening. This was the
exact time that Jesus had told the father to return to his son because
he would live. He rejoiced with his household that Jesus indeed was
the Great Physician. He had put his faith in Jesus when he had told

him, "Your son will live," and his faith had not been put to shame. Jesus' word was true and his response to the man's faith was sure. God rewards those who earnestly seek him.

The effect of this life-saving miracle was that not only did the royal official believe in Jesus but also all the members of his household put their faith in him, including servants and immediate family members. This high-ranking nobleman was able to reach the people who were under him so that in turn they could influence many others in Capernaum and elsewhere.

Application

An age-old adage says, "The family that prays together stays together." And this proverb is still relevant today when our busy schedules compete with daily family devotions. As families, we often fail to bring our needs to God in prayer. We frequently neglect to wait expectantly for him to answer. Often we forget to express thanks to him for answered prayers. The bottom line is that God wants us to come to him in faith with our petitions and with our thankful praise. And we know that he hears us when we ask him in accordance with his will.

The Father of an Epileptic Boy

The Disciples' Failure

Epilepsy is a disease that strikes a person's central nervous system, causing periods of unconsciousness and convulsions. In biblical times, an epileptic was called a lunatic because of the belief that the phases of the moon (*luna,* in Latin) caused his or her behavior. In modern times, medicines prevent such seizures and make it possible for people to lead normal lives, but that was not the case for a certain Galilean boy in Jesus' day who suffered from epileptic fits. His parents surmised that an evil spirit was throwing him to the ground, sometimes into the water and at other times into a fire. If it had not been for his parents' watchful care, the boy would have been killed. They tried everything to find a cure for their child's illness.

Jairus' rank was a little lower than that of a teacher who enjoyed enormous prestige. Nonetheless, he was well respected among the members of the synagogue and had a good name.

Eventually there was joy in the home of Jairus when his wife gave birth to a beautiful girl. As an only child, this girl became the object of much affection in the family. But when she reached the age of twelve, her health suddenly began to deteriorate, and doctors were unable to help her.

When she was near death, her parents could think only of Jesus, who lived in Capernaum and had healed numerous people. Some of these people had been healed in the synagogue even during the worship services. Jairus had witnessed these miracles. A few of the Pharisees had been heard to object to Jesus' healing the sick on the Sabbath, for that meant breaking the law. They had even suggested that he should have waited until the next day and thus avoided desecrating the Sabbath.

But Jairus was unable to locate Jesus, who he was told had left in a fishing boat and had gone to the other side of the Lake of Galilee. He went to the shore to see if Jesus and his disciples were returning to Capernaum. His daughter was desperately ill, and there was no time to lose. If Jesus did not hurry, he might very well be too late to heal his ailing child. Anxiously he scanned the horizon, and then to his relief he saw a boat coming toward shore. And when it came closer, he saw that Jesus was aboard.

As soon as Jesus disembarked, a large crowd surrounded him. It was almost impossible for Jairus to approach Jesus, but eventually he was successful. He fell down before Jesus and implored him to come to his house immediately, for his little daughter was seriously ill and at the point of death. He asked him to lay his hands on his dear child and heal her so that she might live. He knew that Jesus, with his divine healing power, could do this. He had faith in Jesus and trusted him to come without delay.

Jesus consented to come along with him, but with the large crowd stalling him, he failed to make headway. The pressure of this crowd was so intense that they nearly crushed him. Even one woman who had been suffering for many years from a flow of blood touched him and was healed. Jairus had no objection to her being healed, but it took time away from Jesus, who had promised to come to his darling daughter. If there would be any further delay, it might no longer be necessary for Jesus to come to his house.

Indeed, some neighbors of Jairus came with the sad news that his daughter had died. These friends asked why Jairus should continue to bother Jesus. They said that it was too late. The ruler of the synagogue, who had done everything possible to save his daughter's life, was grief-stricken and distraught. Now in the very presence of Jesus, he learned that she was dead.

Overhearing the men talking to Jairus, Jesus addressed him and said, "Don't fear; only believe." Jesus was in charge, and he intimated that Jairus ought to realize he did not have to listen to his friends. Jesus expected Jairus to have faith in him. He told the crowd, Jairus' neighbors, and the disciples that only three of his closest friends (Peter, James, and John) might accompany him into the house.

A Daughter Raised to Life

When they came to the house, the people there were in deep mourning and caused a near tumult with their loud wailing and shedding of tears. Upon entering the house, Jesus asked these people why they were making all that noise and commotion. Obviously such a question was out of place. What else would Jesus expect in a house of death?

Jesus had not seen the girl, had not observed her, and had not drawn the conclusion that she indeed had died. The mourners could forgive Jesus for his seemingly ignorant question. But when he said, "The child is not dead but asleep," the mourners burst out laughing. The switch from mourning to laughing, however, revealed their insincerity. These people were paid to shed tears and expected a handsome remuneration for their services. They knew that the girl had died, and to say that she was asleep was at best naïve. But Jesus used the word *asleep* as a euphemism.

Jesus had little patience with the crowd. He ordered them out of the house, for he did not want anyone near him and the girl, except for the three disciples and her father and mother. He approached the child where she lay on a bed, took her by the hand, and then uttered two words in the Aramaic language spoken by the Jews in Israel. He said, *"Talitha koum."* Translated into English, these words mean, "Little girl, I say to you, get up."

Jesus confronted death in its fullness; his majestic voice of authority addressed its power, and the angel of death obediently released the little girl. He did not speak magical formulas; he merely told her to get up.

The girl's spirit returned. She sat up, stood on her feet, and began to walk. Not surprisingly, the parents and the three disciples were utterly amazed and filled with joy. Tears of sorrow suddenly turned into tears of laughter. Trust and faith in Jesus had paid rich dividends to Jairus and his family.

Jesus instructed the parents to give her something to eat to prove to them that she was back to health and needed nourishment. It also gave Jesus and the disciples a reason for getting away from the people inside the house. He instructed the parents not to let anyone know what had happened. Of course, as soon as Jairus's daughter walked outside, the people would see her and ask what had happened. The parents would never be able to keep this miracle a secret. The purpose for this command was to give Jesus and his disciples sufficient time to leave the crowds in Capernaum behind as they traveled on foot to Nazareth, Jesus' hometown.

Application

The daughter of Jairus was the first of three people whom Jesus brought back to life; the other two were the young man of Nain and Lazarus. But all these people eventually faced death again.

In contrast, Jesus rose from the grave in a transformed body, never to die again. He rose as the firstfruits from the dead. This means that in the day of resurrection, our bodies will rise from the grave and be like Jesus' body. We will be impervious to death and reign with Jesus forever.

A Sick Woman

A Debilitating Malady

A longtime resident of Capernaum had become ill, and all her visits to the doctors failed to restore her health. She kept her illness a secret because it was embarrassing to her and because she would be regarded as unclean, since it involved the loss of blood. She became physically weak, and her complexion was pale and wan. The joy of living had departed from her long ago, and she had become a lonely figure in society.

The woman had gone from one doctor to the next, but their medicines had failed to provide a cure. In the meantime, her medical bills reduced her assets to such a degree that she now belonged to the poverty-stricken class. Her health had been steadily deteriorating for twelve years, and there was no cure in sight.

In her hometown, she had heard that Jesus, the teacher from Nazareth, had healed a number of people in Capernaum, Galilee, and Judea. People with various diseases had come to him, and he had healed them by either speaking a word or touching them.

Even a leper whom no one dared to touch for fear of contamination had come to him. Jesus had reached out his hand to touch him. Then he had said, "Be clean," and at that very moment the man was healed.

Also, Jesus had healed a paralyzed man whose four friends had carried him to the house where Jesus was. They had been unable to approach him because of the crowd, so they had carried the paralytic on his mat up onto the flat roof. They dug a hole through the roof and let the man down right in front of Jesus, who then healed him. Consequently, Jesus became known as the Great Physician.

An Immediate Healing

The woman left her home and walked to the house where she knew Jesus stayed, but when she arrived, she was told that Jesus had gone with his disciples by fishing boat to the other side of the Lake of Galilee. She was disappointed not to find Jesus at home, but she walked over to the shore to see whether a fishing boat might have returned with Jesus and his followers. To her amazement, a boat had docked with Jesus aboard, and he was coming ashore. But almost at once, a crowd of people surrounded him and formed a throng so pressing that it became nearly impossible for her to come near Jesus.

Slowly the multitude moved toward the city. Just then there was an opening that gave the woman the opportunity to come close to Jesus. It was now or never. She did not dare fall at Jesus' feet and ask him personally. She wanted no publicity and preferred to be inconspicuous. Considering her hemorrhage, she regarded herself an unclean woman who would not even be allowed in a crowd. Instead, she wanted to touch the edge of his robe as he walked past, for she said to herself that if she merely touched his clothes, she would be healed. So when Jesus' cloak swung past, she reached out, and one of the tassels at the bottom of his coat brushed over her hand.

Immediately the woman felt a powerful surge enter her body. She knew that her affliction was taken away, the flow of blood was stanched, and she was healed. Her faith in Jesus was fully rewarded right on the spot. Not only was she healed in her body but Jesus also strengthened her spiritually. Her faith, which had brought her into contact with Jesus, was now fortified.

No sooner had she felt his healing power in her body than Jesus turned around and asked the crowd, "Who touched my cloak?"

No one answered because the crowd had been pressing around him. Peter, who always appeared to be the spokesman, remarked that many people were pushing and crowding him. Anyone could have touched him.

Jesus looked around him to see who could have tapped into his source of strength. He said, "Someone touched me, for I know that power has gone out from me." Jesus knew that because of steadfast faith in him, power had left him and gone into someone else for healing. This outflow had not diminished Jesus' ability to heal, but he wanted to address the person who had become its recipient. And he realized that this person was a woman.

Unable to hide, the woman came to him, trembling and falling at his feet. She understood that Jesus was not addressing the crowd but her. She had to confess that she had touched the edge of his cloak. She, who had always practiced modesty and deference, now had to speak up in front of Jesus and the people surrounding him. In public, she had to confess her faith in him and reveal the embarrassing information about her ailment.

Fear and dread caused her to tremble, for she had no idea how Jesus would react and what the people would say about her. Yet when she looked into Jesus' eyes, she was assured that everything was all right. She related what she had done and how she had been healed.

Jesus' response was positive. He kindly addressed her as daughter, even though they were the same age. He said that her faith had healed her. And he told her to go in peace. Jesus used the word *to heal*, which also meant *to save*. Because of her faith, Jesus healed her both physically and spiritually.

Jesus reinstated the woman as a member of the community. And she in turn could testify to others about the all-encompassing healing power of Jesus Christ. She who received a special blessing from heaven now could express her heartfelt thanks to God in heaven. The pathway of blessings was complete. Blessings descended from heaven to earth, and at the same time, thanksgiving ascended from earth to heaven.

Application

Faith triumphs when we are in the will of God. But how do we know we are in his will? The answer is given in the first three petitions of the Lord's Prayer:

- Hallowed be your name.
- Your kingdom come.
- Your will be done on earth as it is in heaven.

When we seek to honor God, when we promote his kingdom, and when we work in loving obedience to do his will, then miracles occur in answer to faith. Then we ask with the right motives and God answers our petitions.

A Paralytic

Fully Dependent on Others

Countless people had heard about Jesus' teaching and healing. Pharisees and those who were called teachers of the law wanted to hear him. They had come from towns and villages throughout Galilee and Judea; some had even come from Jerusalem. They wanted to know if his teaching was in harmony with theirs. And they wanted him to demonstrate his miracle-working power. They entered the home where Jesus was and sat around the walls and on the floor. The house was crowded so that there was no room left, not even around the doorway.

With a captive audience in the house, Jesus took the opportunity to teach the people from the Scriptures. The learned rabbis were ready with their questions and immediately found out that Jesus was fully versed in the Scriptures and from beginning to end knew them by heart. Jesus proved to be an expert teacher who was not at all intimidated by his audience. He was the teacher and they were his students. But would they be able to pass judgment on his power to perform miracles?

In the town of Capernaum lived a man who had been paralyzed and was confined to his mat. If he wanted to go somewhere, four people had to carry him on his pallet, one at each corner. He had heard that Jesus of Nazareth, who had taken up residence in Capernaum, was a healer of those who were sick and afflicted. Numerous people had come to him and Jesus had healed them. Would it be possible for the paralytic to see him and be restored to health? He asked this question of his four friends who often carried him. They decided to carry him to Jesus, and then they would be able to ask him.

The Faith of Five People

The four men carried the paralytic to the house where Jesus stayed. But when they came near, they saw a crowd of people standing outside and in the doorway. They could hear Jesus' voice, but it was impossible to come near him. There simply was no room to approach the teacher.

The men were undaunted; they knew that Jesus had the power to heal. But how would they get close to him? They saw a staircase alongside the house that led to the flat roof. In Israel, roofs of houses were constructed of hardened dirt mixed with straw. This substance was deposited on the crossbeams and branches that formed the ceiling. The four friends took the man on his pallet up the staircase to the roof. At the spot where they heard the sound of Jesus' voice, they dug through the dirt and made a hole. They were careful to gather the dirt on a pile so that it would not fall on Jesus and his listeners. Then they tied ropes to the corners of the pallet and carefully lowered the paralytic right in front of Jesus.

As soon as the hole in the roof appeared, Jesus lost the attention of his audience. Everyone was looking up to see what was happening. When they saw the pallet with the paralytic on it, they had to admire the men for their ingenuity and persistence. Some were amused, others chuckled, and all were waiting to see what Jesus would do. Was this the moment that he would work a miracle right in front of them?

No word needed to be spoken. It was self-evident that the paralytic, who looked up at Jesus, and the four friends on the roof, who looked down at him, were asking Jesus to heal the man. They knew that he could heal by merely speaking a word.

Jesus spoke a short sentence. He said to the paralytic, "Son, your sins are forgiven." These words caused great consternation and confusion, for it was not apparent that the paralytic had offended Jesus, unless he was offended by the interruption of his teaching. But Jesus used the plural form *sins*, which referred to a long list of offenses one had committed against God. Had Jesus been teaching about sin? Had the paralytic sinned against God's law prior to his misfortune? The Gospels are silent on these questions. Significant is the fact that for this miracle to happen, Jesus began with the man's soul and afterward healed his body. Body and soul go together, and of the two, the soul comes first.

Jesus Proves His Divinity

No wonder the religious leaders were upset with Jesus, who put himself on the level of God when he declared that this man's sins were forgiven. Who did this Galilean prophet think he was? This kind of talk was blasphemy. He should know that only God forgives sins. They did not utter a word, but their demeanor spoke volumes. The tension in the room was real. Instead of acknowledging Jesus as a teacher, they now were rejecting him as a blasphemer.

Jesus was aware of their thoughts. He asked them why they were thinking negative thoughts that poisoned the atmosphere and broke the relationship of teacher and listeners. He placed a choice before them. He asked them, "What is easier to say to the paralytic, 'Your sins are forgiven,' or 'Get up, take your pallet, and walk'?" If they chose the first, they would have to agree that Jesus was divine. If they opted for the second, they likewise would have to acknowledge his divinity.

Jesus did not even give them time to answer. He said, "But that you may know that the Son of Man has authority to forgive sins . . ." Then he addressed the paralytic: "I tell you, get up, take your pallet, and go home." At that moment, the miracle happened. The man did what Jesus told him to do. He felt the healing power rush through his lame body, and he could move his legs and arms. He used his arms to push himself up, then stretched his legs and stood. Reaching down, he picked up his pallet and started for home.

The man was healed because he and his four friends had put their trust in Jesus. And Jesus had acknowledged that faith and healed the paralytic. But at the same time, he taught all those who were present that he was indeed divine. The Pharisees and teachers of the law had to admit that Jesus had given them proof of his divinity. Also, all the others who saw the paralytic walking home cried out that they had never seen anything like it. They had seen the glory of God displayed before them all.

Application

The five men showed persistent determination to meet Jesus against all odds and displayed unwavering faith in Jesus. We notice that Jesus honored their faith even though no recorded words were spoken by these men. It is well known that the faith of a righteous person is effective and especially so when a number of believers exercise it jointly.

When fathers and mothers demonstrate their faith in the immediate family circle, the children are able to observe the result of faith that is accompanied by prayer. In addition, this combination of prayer and faith has a wholesome effect on unbelievers. When we ask God in faith to answer our prayers, we will experience that he pours out his blessings upon us and through them is leading unbelievers to himself.

A Sinful Woman

A Sinful Woman Repents

One day Jesus was talking with a prostitute in the courtyard of a well-known Pharisee. This woman was considered to be immoral by the people in her village and the leaders of the synagogue. Because of her conduct, she was excommunicated and barred from attending the worship services on the Sabbath. She was called a sinner, which did not mean that everyone else was without sin, but it conveyed the idea that she lived an immoral life.

Yet this woman hated her debased life. She sought relief from a guilty conscience, knowing that her life was in ruins. She longed for normalcy. She needed someone to lead her to God, to find forgiveness of sin, and to receive the cleansing of her guilty soul. The clergy refused to do anything spiritual for her; they would not even allow her to come to them. The coming of a prostitute to a respected rabbi would be interpreted as solicitation, and that act would increase her guilt.

One Sabbath morning, she wandered toward the synagogue, where the worship service was in progress. She could not enter the building, yet no one could bar her from sitting outside to listen to the preacher. She listened attentively to the words that were flowing from the lips of the speaker.

Jesus called the people in the synagogue to repent of their sins and their wicked ways. He invited them to confess their sins and short-comings to God, and he assured them that God in tender love would graciously forgive them. He told them that God not only would forgive their sins but also would forget them. Anyone who would come to God would never be cast out, for God would forgive and restore this fallen human being.

These words of Jesus touched the woman deeply; she quickly walked away from the synagogue before the service came to an end. But in her home, she fell to her knees and in prayer con-fessed her sinful past to God, who heard her plea for forgiveness and with his Spirit calmed her soul. Heavenly peace entered her inner being and she became filled with a desire to thank Jesus for the words she had heard that morning. She wanted to give him something that was precious to her, namely, an alabaster jar of perfume.

The Aroma of Kindness

The woman knew that a prominent Pharisee named Simon had invited Jesus and other leading people in the community to come to his house for the noon meal that particular Sabbath. Depend-ing on the time of year and weather conditions, the meal would be consumed outdoors in the courtyard of Simon's home. This outdoor event could be observed by anyone in the village, and as was traditional in Jewish society, it was accessible to all. Hence the woman, without anyone to hinder her, could not only observe the host, guests, and servers of food, she could also go right up to Jesus and give him the perfume.

She approached the tables, which were put in a U-shaped forma-tion. Jesus was seated at a table near the end away from the head table. He was reclining on a low bench with his left arm on the table and his feet sticking out away from it.

When the woman came behind Jesus, she could no longer control her emotions, and tears filled her eyes. She kneeled down, and her teardrops fell on his feet. Unable to dry his feet with a towel, she used her loose-hanging hair. That action was taboo, for a woman who let her hair down in public was considered a prostitute who was making herself available. She proceeded to kiss Jesus' feet, and then she took the jar of perfume, broke off the top, and poured its contents on his feet. She could have poured it on Jesus' head, but in her prostrate position, she emptied the bottle on his feet.

When Simon observed these actions, he grumbled loud enough for those nearby to hear him: "If this preacher were a prophet, he would have known who and what kind of woman touched him, for she is a sinful woman." Simon was of the opinion that a man of God ought not to let an immoral woman touch him!

Jesus, however, heard everything the host was saying, proving that he indeed was a prophet who knew not only the spiritual condition of the woman but also the thoughts and attitude of this Pharisee. He called him by name and said, "Simon, I have something to tell you." And Simon responded, "Teacher, say it." The host did not realize that when he asked Jesus to speak, he would become a target.

Jesus told a story of two men who each owed their creditor a sum of money. The one owed five hundred silver coins, and the other fifty. When both of them lacked the resources to pay the creditor back at the appointed time, he canceled their debts. Then Jesus asked Simon, "Which of the two men loved the creditor more?" And the host answered, "I suppose the man who was forgiven the greater debt." Jesus agreed and said, "Right you are."

Jesus had not uttered one word to the woman while he addressed the host. Now looking to Simon and pointing his finger at her, he began to speak to him words of reproof.

The Lesson for Simon

Jesus asked Simon whether he saw the woman, which was a question that needed no answer. He explained that when he came to Simon's house, no one washed his feet. But this woman had washed them with her tears and dried them with her hair. He pointed out that Simon had not welcomed him with a kiss. But she had not stopped kissing his feet from the moment she had arrived. And he said that Simon had neglected to put oil on his guest's head as a token of respect. But this woman had anointed his feet with perfume.

He called attention to the woman's spiritual condition and explained that she was a sinner whose many sins God had forgiven. Jesus then subtly applied the earlier parable to Simon: "But the one who is forgiven little, loves little."

Simon had failed deplorably in every respect as a host. But the woman had served Jesus as hostess. She kissed and anointed his feet. She showed him her profound love for leading her to God. She knew that God had forgiven her and had cleansed her soul. Jesus affirmed this to her by saying, "Your sins have been forgiven."

The lesson Jesus taught Simon was personal and direct, for it conveyed to him that all sinners must come to God in repentance and faith to receive pardon. The guests at the table apparently failed to accept the lesson Jesus had taught. Instead, they scolded him by asking, "Who is this who even forgives sins?" In their opinion, not Jesus but only God could forgive sins. They refused to see that the woman had come to Jesus in faith because God had pardoned her.

Jesus' last words to the woman were filled with love and comfort: "Your faith has saved you; go in peace." Her faith in him brought full restoration of her body and soul. She could now live her life in peace with God and fellow human beings.

Application

The fifth petition in the Lord's Prayer reads, "Forgive us our debts as we also have forgiven our debtors." God forgives our sins and at the same forgets them. Indeed, he remembers our sins no more. But if we refuse to forgive others and nurse our grudges, then God will not forgive us either but will remember our sins.

All sinners need to come to Jesus, who is the fountain that cleanses them from sin and guilt and restores their spiritual lives to God's service.

ZACCHAEUS

A Broken Man's Hope

His father and mother called him Zacchaeus when he was born. The name is a Hebrew term meaning "pure." But Zacchaeus did not appreciate that name at all. When he was growing up, his playmates called him "pure," directly as well as indirectly indicating that he would have to live up to his name. He could not play in the soil and get mud on his clothes or dirt on his hands and face.

When he became an adult, his fellow Jews expected him to be honest, trustworthy, and true to his word. But this was not the case. His one desire in life was to become rich. He found a way to reach that goal in becoming a tax collector on behalf of the occupying Roman forces in Jericho. His job was to collect revenue not only from all of the citizens in that locale but also from the merchants who traveled through it on their way to and from Judea, Samaria, and Galilee.

Collecting taxes implied first that he worked for the hated Roman government and second that the Romans allowed him to pocket a surcharge for his own use. In time, he was appointed chief tax collector, which meant that he collected funds from all of his underlings. Zacchaeus became rich, bought a luxurious home in the Roman part of the city, and lived in comfort and ease.

On his way to Jerusalem, Jesus decided to find accommodations in Jericho. He did so by looking up into a sycamore tree, where he saw a lonely figure hiding among the leaves. Surrounded by a throng of people, he stopped right under the tree and called out, "Zacchaeus, come down quickly, for I must stay at your house today."

Zacchaeus was short, which by itself was enough to give him an inferiority complex, but he also was shunned by the people for his occupation. The religious authorities had excommunicated him from the synagogue and considered him an outcast. His conscience bothered him, and he knew that he was a sinner in the presence of God and his fellow man. But he was unable to find spiritual help.

He had heard Jesus teach at one time or other and had found comfort in his message of repentance and spiritual restoration. He longed to hear Jesus again and decided that if there ever came an opportunity to ask him questions, he would talk to him.

When Zacchaeus heard that Jesus was coming through the city of Jericho as a wayfarer, he knew that the day had come to talk to Jesus. But when he heard the crowds of people coming toward him, Zacchaeus knew that because of his height he would be unable to see Jesus. And because of his occupation, he was afraid to mingle with the crowd. The safest place to observe Jesus was in a sycamore tree, even though that would not bring him close to Jesus and he also would probably have to endure the unkind remarks of teenagers, who would ridicule an older man for climbing the tree as if he were one of them. But Zacchaeus was willing to risk their abusive language.

Zacchaeus' Place

What a surprise, and at the same time, what an embarrassment! Jesus stopped, looked up into the tree, and gazed into Zacchaeus' eyes. There was no escape, for Jesus called him by name and told him not only to come down but also to be his host. How did he know his name? He did not scold him for his conduct in society, did not reject him, did not say anything about his excommunication from the synagogue, and did not tell him to repent. He said that Zacchaeus had to come down immediately from the sycamore tree because Jesus was going to stay in his house that day.

Zacchaeus would have to entertain Jesus and his twelve disciples in his home and lodge them for the night. What would the people in Jericho think of Jesus' staying in the home of a tax collector? Would they not say that a holy man of God ought not to mingle with sinners such as a chief tax collector? Not only the religious leaders but also all the people took offense. All of them had been duped by the chief tax collector, and his pockets were filled with their money.

Without delay, Zacchaeus slid down the sycamore tree and stood before Jesus. He knew at once that Jesus was not ashamed to come to his abode and to associate with him. He was filled with joy, for he had much to tell the great teacher. He had to speak words that came from the bottom of his heart, words that he was unable to utter in the presence of the Jewish clergy, for they refused to listen to him. But here in the presence of Jesus he was given the freedom to speak about his life, which had been spent in pursuit of worldly possessions. He realized that he had been set free from this pursuit, and he wanted to tell Jesus and all the people about his freedom.

Zacchaeus knew in his heart that money no longer held him in its grip, for it had lost all of its appeal. He wanted to get rid of it as soon as possible and put it in the hands of people who needed it most, those who were poverty-stricken. Standing before Jesus with a crowd of people listening, he said,

- "Look, Lord, half of my possessions I'll give to the poor."
- "If I have cheated anyone out of anything, I'll pay him back four times as much."

That would leave him little more than a bare subsistence. With half of his possessions given away, many claimants would be at his door cashing in on the generous retribution Zacchaeus offered them from the other half.

Old Testament law stipulated that whenever money was taken illegally, the offender would have to return the full amount plus 20 percent. Zacchaeus was willing to pay back the full amount plus 300 percent to show repentance and express gratitude to Jesus. His gratitude was a demonstration of faith in Jesus and of his willingness to make himself a servant. Jesus did not ask him to give up his possessions, nor did he tell him to leave his occupation. Zacchaeus' decision to part with his wealth was voluntary and proof that he now wished to serve Jesus.

Jesus responded to Zacchaeus in the hearing of the crowd: "Today salvation has come to this house, because also this man is a son of Abraham; for the Son of Man came to seek and to save that which is lost." By birth, Zacchaeus was a son of Abraham, but Jesus called him a spiritual son. He could now claim spiritual sonship in the lineage of Abraham. Jesus said to Zacchaeus that he had to be in his house today. This means that Zacchaeus and his household came to faith in Jesus and were now members of the household of faith.

Application

Salvation and healing go hand in hand, for God saves completely and at the same time restores the sinner in relation to himself and to full acceptance in the Christian community. Salvation can be gained only when a sinner expresses faith in Jesus Christ, who in response forgives sin and opens the way to God.

Hence, salvation is a gift of God to a forgiven sinner, who is a brand plucked from the fire and who becomes a useful servant, living a life of thankfulness.

People Whom Jesus Healed

Bartimaeus

Matthew 20, Mark 10, and Luke 18

Along the Jericho Road

The name Bartimaeus is a combination of the Aramaic word *bar* ("son") and the Greek term *timaeus* ("the honorable one"). Both the Aramaic and Greek languages were spoken in Jericho, where Bartimaeus lived. His family was thoroughly acquainted with Jewish culture, language, and traditions, while at the same time Greek civilization and the Greek language had a profound influence on their lives. Aramaic was spoken in the home.

Although the Jews lived in old Jericho, which they considered their city, the Romans had built their administrative center adjacent to it. In this center, the chief tax collector, Zacchaeus, lived, away from the Jews who despised him for being in the employ of Rome. Coming from the Jordan on his way to Jerusalem, Jesus had to go through old Jericho and then through its administrative center.

Along the road between the city and the administrative center sat Bartimaeus, who, because he was blind, had no employment and had to beg. This was common in those regions where eye care was elementary and diseases rampant. Blindness struck both young and old.

Bartimaeus had heard about Jesus of Nazareth and knew that this prophet had performed many miracles, among them giving sight to the blind. While he sat by the road, he heard the voices of a crowd coming toward him. These people were on their way to Jerusalem for the celebration of the Passover Feast. As he heard them talk about Jesus, Bartimaeus realized that the prophet of Nazareth was in their midst.

Receiving Sight

Bartimaeus understood that his opportunity to receive sight had come. All he had to do was call out the name of Jesus, who, in his mind, was none other than the Messiah, and he would receive sight. He knew this for a fact. Seven centuries earlier, the prophet Isaiah had prophesied that when the Messiah, the Son of David, came, he would give sight to the blind. In all of history, no physician in Israel had been able to restore sight to the blind. But Jesus of Nazareth had healed a number of blind people, and therefore, in the mind of Bartimaeus, Jesus was the Son of David, the fulfiller of Scripture's prophecies.

Bartimaeus called out, "Jesus, Son of David, have mercy on me!" He said it over and over until the people near him had more than enough and told him to be quiet. The blind man, however, refused to be silent and continued to call on Jesus for help.

Jesus heard the blind man's call and stopped. He was not pleased with the bystanders who had rebuked the man. Jesus wanted them to become his willing servants who would submit to his authority. He told them to call Bartimaeus. And so they did, for their rebuke turned into words of encouragement. They said to the blind man, "Cheer up, arise, for he is calling you!"

Bartimaeus responded by throwing his cloak aside so as not to be impeded; he stood up and walked toward Jesus. Bystanders now were willing to help him by taking his hand and leading him to Jesus. Then he heard Jesus asking him, "What do you want me to do for you?" He blurted out, "Rabbouni, that I may see." He addressed Jesus not with the term *Rabbi* but with the title *Rabbouni* in his native Aramaic.

Jesus' response was short and to the point. In Galilee, he had touched another man's eyes with saliva, but to Bartimaeus he only spoke the words, "Go, your faith has healed you," and he was healed. His eyes could see as darkness turned to light. Bartimaeus could set eyes on Jesus, the bystanders, the blue sky, the white clouds, and the green grass and trees.

Bartimaeus's days of begging for alms had come to an end, for now he could assume a normal life in society. He joined the crowd following Jesus on the road into the new Jericho. Bartimaeus followed Jesus by glorifying God for granting him the healing miracle of sight. Likewise, all the people who had seen Jesus perform this miracle now praised God as they continued their travels to Jerusalem.

Bartimaeus was healed because of his faith in Jesus, the Messiah, who had fulfilled the scriptural prophecies of giving sight to the blind. His persistent calling on Jesus brought amazing results, for Jesus never turned away people who came to him in faith and perseverance. By rewarding the blind man's faith in the Son of David and restoring his sight at once, Jesus demonstrated to the crowd that he indeed was the Messiah.

Application

The Jewish people knew from Old Testament prophecies that when the Messiah came, he would open the eyes of the blind. Jesus came and by healing the blind proved that he was the Messiah. Jesus healed both physical and spiritual blindness, for he is and remains the Great Physician.

Jesus still heals people physically through today's medical knowledge, instruments, and prescriptions. But he also restores people to spiritual health through the power of his Word and the working of the Holy Spirit. He opens the eyes of spiritually blind people and makes them see him as their Savior.

A Man Born Blind

Washing Mud from His Eyes

Losing one's eyesight later in life is dreadful, but being born blind is far worse. Being blind since birth means missing out on a world filled with color and beauty.

Such was the life of a particular man born in the city of Jerusalem. When he was a baby, his parents immediately noticed that he was blind. They undoubtedly asked themselves why this had come upon them. But they could not answer this question, and they resigned themselves to caring for a child who would need help for the rest of his life.

There was one redeeming factor in this tragedy: the child was extremely bright. Even though he could not see, his memory was phenomenal and he learned quickly. Yet in those days, the drawback was that when he grew up, he could never be gainfully employed. All he could do was sit along the road and beg. And this is exactly what he did.

When the blind man sat near the temple, he could hear the debates of the Pharisees, scribes, and teachers of the law. He could hear them read and recite Scripture. And with his keen mind, he committed to memory large portions of the Scriptures. He also learned that Jesus of Nazareth taught the fulfillment of many of the biblical prophecies. At times, Jesus preached to the crowds in the temple area called Solomon's Colonnade, where a multitude gathered to hear him. The blind man had been there and had listened to this Galilean preacher.

One day he heard Jesus and his disciples coming near him. He heard them ask Jesus, "Rabbi, who sinned, this man or his parents, that he was born blind?" They seemed to think that because he was blind, his hearing was also impaired. But because of his blindness, his sense of hearing was finely tuned.

Why would the disciples think that the sin of either him or his parents was the cause of his blindness? His parents were upright people who faithfully attended the worship services at the synagogue. And he was unaware of having committed an appalling sin. It was indeed wonderful to hear Jesus' answer that he and his parents were not at fault. Jesus said that he was blind so that God's work might be displayed in his life. He wondered what that might be, for these words were somewhat mysterious. What would God do in his life?

Jesus said, "Night is coming, when no one can work. As long as I am in the world, I am the light of the world." Though the blind man had never seen the light of day, he could feel the warmth of the sun beginning at daybreak and ending at sunset. What did Jesus mean by saying that he was the light of the world? Would he give him sight?

Before the man could reflect on these questions, he heard Jesus spit on the ground to make sticky mud. Then he felt Jesus putting this mud on his eyelids and heard Jesus tell him to go to the Pool of Siloam and wash away the mud. Of course he would go to this pool to cleanse his eyelids, for the mud caked them completely shut. In a sense, he was now twice blind: born blind and prevented from seeing.

He knew exactly where the Pool of Siloam was located in the southeast corner of Jerusalem. The blind man went and did what Jesus told him to do. In childlike obedience, he fully trusted Jesus and washed away the dirt. He opened his eyelids and for the first time saw the water and the stone wall surrounding the pool. He looked and saw people; he put familiar voices together with the faces he saw. He saw trees and green leaves, a blue sky and fluffy white clouds.

The well-known surroundings took on a new dimension. Now the man was able to put sounds and sights together. He jumped for joy and ran home to his parents to see them and to relate what had happened. They rejoiced with him, for they realized that Jesus had performed a wonderful miracle.

The neighbors and others who knew the man looked at him and asked themselves whether he indeed was the one who used to beg along the streets of Jerusalem. Some said that he was the blind man because his facial expressions were the same and so was his clothing. But others were not so sure and said in disbelief that he resembled the man born blind. However, he told the people that he indeed was the former blind beggar.

Some of these people remained unconvinced and demanded to know how he had received his sight. He informed them that the man called Jesus of Nazareth had put mud on his eyes and had told him to wash them in the Pool of Siloam, and that when he had done that, his eyes were opened and he could see. Then they wanted to know where Jesus was, but he was unable to tell them.

Sabbath-Day Questions

It happened to be the Sabbath day and the religious leaders were readily available. So the people went to the Pharisees to ask what this healing could mean in light of the Scriptures. They had heard the term *Son of David*, which was another name for the Messiah. Could it be that this Jesus was indeed the Messiah? Certainly their religious experts should be able to give them a satisfactory answer.

Unfortunately, the Pharisees, scribes, and teachers of the law were not concerned with the question of whether the Messiah had arrived among them. They were upset about the work that Jesus had done by healing on the Sabbath. They said that this teacher from Nazareth was guilty of Sabbath desecration. The rabbis had made it known that if someone's eye was inflamed and the person was in pain, then ointment might be applied to relieve the discomfort. But the man born blind had not suffered from any painful inflammation. The healing could have waited until the next day.

The religious leaders asked the man to relate in detail what had happened and what Jesus had done to him. They were strict legalists who applied their man-made laws to observing the Sabbath properly. They had formulated hundreds of laws on what may or may not be done on the Sabbath. They faulted Jesus for not observing their regulations, yet they absolved the blind man of complicity. These scribes and Pharisees refused to utter Jesus' name but called him "this man." They even went so far as to say that "this man" was not from God because he had desecrated the Sabbath.

Yet other Pharisees, among them perhaps Nicodemus, disagreed. In defense of Jesus, they said that if he were a sinner who broke the law of the Sabbath, he certainly would not be able to perform miracles. The undeniable fact of the blind man's healing indicated that God had empowered Jesus. As a result, the religious officials were divided and failed to agree on acknowledging Jesus as one who was sent and empowered by God.

The disbelieving Pharisees turned to the man who had been healed and demanded that he identify Jesus. They asked him, "What do you say about him because he opened your eyes?" They forced the man to take sides: be either for or against Jesus!

The man answered the Pharisees lucidly: "He is a prophet." He could have said, "The Prophet," namely, the Messiah. But he refrained from elaborating and merely identified Jesus as a prophet. For him, a man who had the power to perform this miracle had to have divine authority and had to be a prophet. Jesus was a man whom God had sent.

The Pharisees refused to accept the man's testimony. As a last resort, they decided to interview his parents. They reasoned that his father and mother would be able to supply them with correct answers and that with these they could prove that their colleagues were incorrect. His parents could testify to the fact that their son was born blind and could report how he was healed.

Accusations Disguised as Questions

Someone was sent to locate the man's parents and summon them to the meeting place, much the same as if they were dragged into court to testify on oath. The leaders presented them with three questions:

- "Is this your son?"
- "Was he born blind?"
- "How then does he now see?"

The parents readily answered the first two questions but realized the danger of answering the third. Of course their son had told them that Jesus had performed the miracle of healing his blindness. But they knew that by telling the Pharisees, they would be in danger of being banned from the services in their synagogue. The Pharisees had made it known that anyone who acknowledged that Jesus was the Messiah would be excluded from the synagogue.

The parents of the man born blind responded to the question, "How then does he now see?" by saying that they did not know and that the religious leaders should ask their son. For good measure, they added that he was of age, that he could speak for himself. They did not want to get involved in a religious dispute with the Pharisees, so they placed their son in a predicament.

The religious leaders once more turned to the man who was born blind and said to him, "Give glory to God." This did not mean, "Praise the Lord," but was the equivalent of putting the man under oath in a court of law. The Pharisees were convinced that the man had not told them everything he knew. They could excuse his parents, for they had not been present when their son received his sight. But the man who once was blind and now could see had to tell them the truth.

They did not ask the man whether Jesus was the Messiah. Instead they came with a blunt statement: "We know that this man [Jesus] is a sinner." They implied that Jesus, whose name they refused to utter, was a sinner because he desecrated the Sabbath.

The man whom Jesus healed refused to join in a debate on Sabbath legalities and pointedly told the prosecuting attorneys that he did not know whether Jesus was a sinner. He said he knew full well that whereas he was blind, he now could see. The prosecutors came right back to him with two questions:

- "What did he do to you?"
- "How did he open your eyes?"

These were loaded questions, which the man, with remarkable wit, sidestepped. He said, "I told you already but you didn't listen. Why do you want to hear it again and again? You don't want to become his disciples too, do you?" By listening to the Pharisees and teachers of the law debate one another during his many years of blindness, the man had developed reasoning skills. And now fully acquainted with their expertise, he met them on their own turf.

The man's last question stung them, and they began to insult him. They said, "You are a disciple of that fellow, but we are disciples of Moses. We know that God has spoken to Moses, but we don't know where this fellow is from." Again they refused to utter Jesus' name and contemptuously referred to him as "this fellow."

A Clever Refutation

The man who had been healed by Jesus knew the Scriptures and had memorized significant passages, especially the messianic prophecies. He learned from the Book of Isaiah that the Messiah at his coming would give sight to the blind.

Throughout history not one person had ever been healed of blindness, and certainly not anyone who had been born blind. Now Jesus had come to this man who was born blind and had granted him the gift of sight. Therefore, the man not only confessed Jesus as the Messiah, but he used this scriptural knowledge to put his prosecutors to shame. He said, "Now this is remarkable indeed!" and then stated his first proposition:

- "You say that you do not know where he comes from, but he opened my eyes."
- "We know that God does not listen to sinners."

Next, he stated his second proposition:

- "If this Jesus fears God and does his will, God listens to him."
- "We have never heard of someone opening the eyes of a person born blind."

And last he drew his conclusion:

- "If this Jesus were not from God, he would not be able to do anything."

He intimated that they should check for themselves the prophecies of Isaiah predicting that when the Messiah came, he would open the eyes of the blind. Now the Messiah had indeed arrived in the person of Jesus, for he had opened the blind man's eyes.

The religious leaders were unable to refute the man's logic. However, they refused to open their spiritual eyes to see the fulfillment of the Scripture in Jesus. Again they resorted to insult and ridicule. They retorted that the man was born blind because at the moment of birth he already was polluted by sin. They implied that he was a sinner from the moment he was born and therefore could not be a member of the synagogue. He had to be expelled, excluded, and ostracized. Their vicious attack showed they acknowledged that he was born blind, but they rejected the plain truth that Jesus had given him sight. Thus, the man was ousted because of his faith in Jesus.

The news about the man's expulsion from the synagogue spread like wildfire throughout the city. When Jesus heard about it, he went to look for the man he had healed

When Jesus found his disciple, he asked him, "Do you believe in the Son of Man?" The blind man healed by Jesus had earlier heard his voice but had never seen him. Now by putting voice and face together, he recognized Jesus as his benefactor. But the question that Jesus posed puzzled him, for he wanted Jesus to explain the term *Son of Man*. He responded by asking, "And who is he, Lord, that I may believe in him?"

Jesus did not give the man a theological lecture to explain his divinity and humanity but simply told him that the one whom he saw and heard talking to him was indeed Jesus, the Son of Man and the Son of God. Jesus asked him whether he had faith in the Messiah, and the man responded, "Lord, I believe!" Now face-to-face with Jesus, the man openly testified to his faith in him.

Jesus pointed out that the one whom God had sent into the world had divine power and authority to pass judgment on unbelievers, including the religious leaders of that day. He uttered his words in the presence of some of the Pharisees. His comment evoked an immediate reaction from them. They asked Jesus, "Are you saying that we are blind, too?" In their opinion, his remark was a slanderous accusation. In their self-centeredness, they claimed that they had perfect eyesight, but they failed miserably in seeing that Jesus was fulfilling Old Testament messianic prophecies.

Jesus replied, "If you were blind, but you deny it, you would have no sin, but in fact you do. Now that you say that you are able to see, your sin remains with you." Jesus came to forgive sin and redeem his people from its bondage. But when the religious leaders willfully rejected him after they had seen with their physical eyes what he had done to the man born blind, they would have to remain in their sin.

Application

Jesus clearly teaches that if we have come to know the truth of God's Word and afterward willfully reject it, we have sinned against the Holy Spirit. And he says that sins committed against the Holy Spirit cannot be forgiven in this life or in the life to come. The teachers of Scripture in Jesus' day should have been the first to acknowledge that he had come as the Messiah. But even when the people were asking them whether Jesus was the Son of David, they refused to accept him as the Messiah but called him Beelzebub, that is, Satan. They were spiritually blind. Anyone who rejects Jesus will be rejected in the presence of God and the holy angels.

A Crippled Woman

LUKE 13

Bent Over in Bondage

Luke, the writer of the Gospel of Luke and the book of Acts, was a doctor by profession and wrote like a physician who provides details of those who are ill. For instance, he noted that the right hand of a man was shriveled, that Peter's mother-in-law had a high fever, and that a woman had a flow of blood for twelve years.

He also described a woman who was crippled by an evil spirit for eighteen years. This woman suffered much. She was bent over and could not straighten up. She was able to walk but constantly had difficulty keeping her balance to avoid stumbling. She was living in a prison from which there was no escape. In addition, because of her physical condition, people regarded her as a pathetic figure on the fringes of society.

As an attendant at the worship services in the synagogue, she was present Sabbath after Sabbath. She enjoyed listening to the scribes who taught lessons from the Scriptures. At one of the services, Jesus was invited to teach a lesson. He taught in such a way that the people were spellbound. He opened the Word of God and taught them the riches of salvation, especially when he selected a messianic passage and expounded on it.

In her bent-over position, the woman had difficulty lifting her head to focus on Jesus, but she noticed that during his lesson, he looked at her from time to time. Could it be that he would work one of his healing miracles on her? She had heard of many other people who had been afflicted physically, and in the last couple of years, Jesus had healed them all. She longed to live a normal life and silently prayed for healing. But in her condition, and as a woman, she could hardly come near him.

Standing Straight

When the lesson was over, Jesus looked at her and in a clear voice asked her to come to him. After she had approached him, he said to her, "Woman, you are set free and remain free from your ailment." In Mideastern culture, to address a female with the word *woman* was customary, polite, and in line with the norms of that day. Jesus spoke this word of healing, laid his hands on her, and set her free from the evil spirit.

Immediately she could straighten herself up to her normal height and in response praised God for the healing that had taken place in her body. She extolled the name of God for all to hear. By speaking to her, Jesus had lifted her up and restored her. She ascribed to him glory and honor.

The people in the synagogue were amazed at what had happened and were rejoicing with the woman at the marvelous work God had performed in their midst. Yet not everyone was happy with Jesus. The ruler of the synagogue was indignant because Jesus had desecrated the Sabbath by doing a work of healing on the day of rest.

If the woman had been in pain because of an inflammation that needed immediate medical attention, Jesus would have been permitted to heal her and thus show mercy. People were permitted to perform works of necessity and mercy on the Sabbath. But these two exceptions did not apply in this case. The synagogue ruler reasoned that Jesus should have waited until the Sabbath had ended, and then he could freely administer his healing power. As a leader, he felt that it was his duty to admonish the worshipers.

Keeping the Sabbath Holy

During his ministry, Jesus taught a fundamental rule: "The Sabbath was made for man, not man for the Sabbath. So the Son of Man is Lord even of the Sabbath." But the clergy had formulated numerous rules and regulations for keeping the Sabbath holy, with the result that life had become unbearable for the people.

God had instituted the law of the Sabbath so that both people and domesticated animals might have one day a week to rest and be refreshed. The religious leaders in Jesus' day enforced this law negatively by stressing what a person might not do. However, Jesus interpreted the same law positively by stressing the joy and happiness that resulted from fulfilling the law. The woman who had been healed demonstrated that joy, and so did the worshipers who witnessed the marvelous thing Jesus did.

As Lord of the Sabbath, Jesus had to correct the synagogue ruler and, by implication, the Pharisees and teachers of the law. He called them hypocrites who taught the people to observe laws that they themselves skirted. Jesus gave them an example. They would take their animals (oxen and donkeys) from their stalls to lead them to the watering trough on the Sabbath. They did not apply the law to themselves and to their animals but untied them to give them water.

They would argue that this work was necessary for the well-being of the animals. Jesus would concur. But for that same reason should not this woman, who was a spiritual and physical daughter of Abraham, be set free from the bondage in which Satan had held her for eighteen years? Should she not be set free on the Sabbath and be given cause for rejoicing?

Jesus took this illustration from daily life and argued from the lesser (the animals) to the greater (the woman). He asked, "If you restrict an animal in a stall for a few hours on the Sabbath but set it free to drink, should an evil spirit be allowed to bind a daughter of Abraham for eighteen years and not be told to release her?"

The religious authorities lacked the spiritual insight to see the battle lines drawn between God's kingdom of light and Satan's kingdom of darkness. Jesus cast out the demons that Satan had ordered to bind God's people, and that included the woman, whom Jesus called a daughter of Abraham. She was a worthy citizen in God's kingdom of light, an honorable member of the household of faith, and a valiant warrior in the army of the Lord.

The ruler of the synagogue and those who supported him had been trying to put Jesus to shame in front of the congregation. When Jesus had appropriately addressed the religious leaders, they lost the respect of the people and were put to shame. On that particular Sabbath, he proclaimed freedom by healing one of God's children.

Jesus had many conflicts with synagogue rulers, Pharisees, and scribes over Sabbath observances. His disciples, walking through a grain field on the Sabbath, picked a few ears of grain, rubbed them to release the kernels, and ate them. According to Sabbath rules, the disciples had desecrated the Sabbath because they had harvested the grain and threshed the ears. On the Sabbath, Jesus healed many people who had physical ailments. He sent a man born blind to the Pool of Siloam to receive his sight. He restored the health of the man at the Pool of Bethesda. And in the house of a prominent Pharisee, Jesus healed a man who was suffering from dropsy. In all these cases, Jesus fulfilled the Law of God and at the same time restored the intent of Sabbath observance, namely, to rejoice in the Lord.

Application

Sunday is a day of revitalization and relaxation for everyone. It is a day in which people are set free from the burdens of their daily labors. As Christians, we spend it doing that which delights and pleases the Lord. Sunday is called the Lord's Day, which means that it belongs to our Lord Jesus Christ.

We worship him, meet together with his people, learn what the Bible teaches about salvation, and participate in Christian fellowship. It is the day when we sing our praises, thank God for granting us spiritual and material blessings, present to him our prayers and petitions, receive the sacraments of baptism and communion, and with our gifts support the poor and the work of the church.

An Invalid

The Pool of Bethesda

We often associate physical healing with pools of water, like Bethesda in ancient Jerusalem and Lourdes in France. Whether people are healed in these waters remains debatable. Often there is a measure of superstition associated with these spas. This is evident in the account of a man who had been paralyzed for thirty-eight years in Jerusalem.

He was a native of Jerusalem, but he belonged to those people who were blind, lame, crippled, and paralyzed. Some said that he was a paralytic, while others were calling him a cripple. Regardless of the ailment, he had been afflicted for decades. He was emaciated, weak, and dependent on the daily care provided by relatives and friends. Physicians were unable to help him, so every day his friends laid him alongside the Pool of Bethesda.

The Pool of Bethesda was in the northeastern part of the old city of Jerusalem near the Sheep Gate and was known for its five covered colonnades. In Aramaic, the word *Bethesda* means "house of mercy," and the pool was reputed to have therapeutic power. Due to internal pressure, the water in the pool stirred from time to time. It was rumored that an angel came down to stir the water and effect healing. Sick people would lie next to the pool in the shade of the porches, waiting for the water to stir. When this disturbance took place, so the sick were told, the first person to enter the water would be healed of his malady.

An Unexpected Cure

Jesus had come to Jerusalem for the celebration of one of the feasts. If it was the Passover, it would have been in the month of March or April. While in Jerusalem, Jesus walked to the Pool of Bethesda, where he saw a withered man lying next to the water. He was told that the man had been in this gaunt condition for thirty-eight years.

Jesus asked the man if he would like to be healed. He responded that there was no one to help him into the pool when the water was stirred. Obviously, his strength was limited, and usually others got there ahead of him.

Then Jesus said to him, "Arise! Take your mattress and walk!" Suddenly he felt strength return to his limbs and surge through his body. He had no difficulty sitting up, then standing; he rolled up his mattress and with a thankful glance in the direction of Jesus, who had turned and left, he began to walk and went on his way home filled with joy.

He had not gone very far when some members of the clergy stopped him. They told him that because it was the Sabbath day, the law prohibited him from carrying his mattress. Carrying anything on the Sabbath was regarded as work and therefore was forbidden. But in the man's opinion, carrying his mattress home was no burden at all. It was a joy to him, for he had been unable to do this for decades. He was taken by surprise. He stammered, "The man who healed me told me to take my mattress and walk." Apparently he did not know Jesus' name, and Jesus had slipped away and could not be found anywhere.

The one-time invalid's answer caused the religious leaders to question him about the person who had made him well. "Who is the man who told you to pick it up and walk?" They were not interested in hearing about the miracle of healing but wanted to find out who had ordered him to break the Sabbath law. They accused not the man who was healed but Jesus for healing the man and thus desecrating the Sabbath.

A Strange Finale

Later that day, Jesus met the Bethesda man walking around in the temple area relatively close to the pool. Jesus had a brief word for him: "Look, you are well now. Stop sinning so that nothing worse may happen to you." He called attention to the man's physical condition, which was back to normal. He also pointed out his spiritual state, which caused him to live a life separated from God and his Word.

Jesus commanded him to refrain from sin; he wanted him to show genuine repentance. If the man kept on living in sin, he certainly would risk acquiring a malady worse than his earlier affliction. On the other hand, it is possible that his misery had been the result of a particular sin that Jesus now wanted him to stop. In short, Jesus called him to repent and follow him with heart, soul, and mind.

The man might not have meant to impede Jesus' work, but he went to the religious leaders to answer the question they had asked earlier. He informed them that Jesus was the one who had healed him and made him well. Unintentionally, he contributed to the Pharisees' opposition to Jesus. The religious leaders confronted Jesus and held him accountable for telling the man to pick up his mattress and walk. But Jesus effectively explained to them that both his Father and he were continuing to perform works of mercy, and that included healing an invalid on the Sabbath.

Application

Jesus showed the man kindness by healing him and told him to stop sinning lest something worse should happen to him. He implied that the man needed to turn his life over to God. Should he ignore

Jesus' admonition, he would risk being spiritually cut off from God and consigned to hell.

Jesus wants us to express our thankfulness to him by living our lives in harmony with God's will. This is a matter not merely of politeness but of worship. As God's children, we should daily thank our heavenly Father for his goodness and provision.

The Young Man of Nain

Sorrow on the Way

Death is all around us. Every tombstone is a monument to sorrow, and every obituary hides a flood of tears. There seems to be no end in sight. When Jesus walked along the roads of Galilee, he often saw the ravages of death, such as in the case of the young man of Nain.

This man's father had passed away when he was still a child. His mother showered him with love and affection and protected him from harm. She never remarried. When he became a teenager, he found employment to bring in much-needed income and defray their living expenses. He and his mother were well known and appreciated in the little town of Nain, which was two miles from Mount Tabor to the southeast of Nazareth.

The Old Testament and the Gospels repeatedly refer to the suffering, abuse, oppression, and injustice endured by widows. Widows lived at the rough edge of poverty, surviving from one day to the next. But God ordained that widows in Israel should receive protection and care. And he said that those who were exploited would find him to be their protector.

One day, the widow's son became ill, and in a relatively short period, he died. She was devastated, for now she had to cope without her son as the breadwinner. The townspeople came to express their condolences and to grieve with her. They accompanied her to the burial site outside the town. Half a dozen young men carried the bier on which the deceased was placed. When they came to the city gate, they noticed that Jesus and his disciples were approaching their town.

Jesus stopped the procession and asked the widow and the accompanying mourners what had happened. When he heard that her only son had died and that she was now alone, he was filled with compassion. Jesus told her not to cry any longer.

But how could she refrain from weeping when her world seemed to have come to an end? She faced a bleak future, for the joy of life had departed from her. Why would God take away first her husband and then her only son? Why continue living when her purpose for life had vanished? She knew that soon after the funeral, her relatives and friends would forget that she was a sorrowing widow with no one to support and comfort her.   *Cmp naomi*

Mourning Turned to Laughter

Jesus knew her thoughts. He walked up to the bier and touched it. Then he addressed the corpse in a clear voice for all to hear: "Young man, I tell you, get up." To everyone's amazement, the dead man heard Jesus' voice, obeyed, and sat up. He opened his mouth, began to talk, and indicated that he had come back from the dead. Then Jesus addressed his mother and told her that she had her son back healthy and well.

The pallbearers, relatives, and friends in the procession were stunned. They had never seen anything like it, nor could anyone recall that a dead person had come back to life. Yet they knew that centuries earlier some people had been raised from the dead. They sensed that this miracle was an act of God, for only the Almighty could accomplish what had occurred among them. From time to time, God had heard their prayers for healing, and the sick became well again. But no one had expected that a dead man on the way to a burial site would sit up, talk, and prove that he was alive. This miracle definitely was exceptional.

The crowd realized that a great prophet had come among them. From their history, they had learned that both Elijah and Elisha were prophets who had worked miracles and had brought dead people to life. And now Jesus of Nazareth had come to Nain to raise one of their young men.

The people knew from the Old Testament that God would swallow up death forever and that he would wipe away the tears from every face (Isa. 25:8). This prophecy was now fulfilled in their little town, because death had lost its power over one of their own citizens.

At the end of time, death shall be no more when Jesus will have triumphed over all of his enemies, of which the last one is death. Then Jesus will shepherd his people and lead them to springs of living water. All of God's people will then surround the throne and every tear will be wiped from their eyes (Rev. 7:17; 21:4). The signs of death, mourning, crying, and pain will all belong to the past, for the old order will have passed away.

Application

No one can escape death, for even those people who returned from death in Jesus' day eventually were again overtaken by it. Paul writes that the last enemy to be destroyed is death and notes that Jesus Christ is victorious over death and the grave.

We share in that conquest over Satan, death, hell, and the grave. God grants this victory to us through his Son, Jesus Christ (1 Cor. 15:55–57). And through the power of Christ, already in this life we enjoy a foretaste of our resurrection.

Martha, Mary, and Lazarus

JOHN 11

Answering the Call of Friends

Less than two miles to the east of Jerusalem was the little village of Bethany, where two sisters and a brother lived. They were Martha, Mary, and Lazarus, dear friends of Jesus. Often when he went to Jerusalem for one of the feasts, he would visit his friends in Bethany and stay with them.

Some time before Jesus' last week on earth, he decided to stay with his disciples on the east side of the Jordan in the region of Perea. The Jewish authorities increasingly threatened his life in Judea, but across the Jordan, he felt relatively safe.

While Jesus was there, he received a message from Mary and Martha that their brother, Lazarus, was sick and had taken a turn for the worse. They urged him to come immediately to Bethany to heal their beloved brother, his dear friend. The sisters realized that it would take a day for him to travel to their home, so their request was urgent: "Jesus, come before it is too late!"

Jesus faced the dilemma of either staying on the east side of the Jordan in relative security or going to Bethany to be captured within sight of Jerusalem. He did not immediately respond to their request but told his disciples that the malady Lazarus suffered would not result in death. He said that God's glory would be revealed in his Son because of Lazarus. He spoke from divine knowledge and implicitly divulged that

- Lazarus would die,
- be raised from the dead,
- and exhibit God's glory.

The miracle of Lazarus's resurrection would reveal that Jesus indeed had divine power.

Jesus decided to stay in Perea two more days. Though he led his disciples to believe that Lazarus's illness was not life-threatening, the disciples had qualms about Jesus' delay in traveling to Bethany. But they could see that ensuring his safety was a valid reason, and they reasoned that he was correct to deny the request of the sisters.

But Jesus had not said that he would not go to Bethany. He indicated only that God would display his glory. Therefore, after two days, Jesus suggested to his disciples that it was time to go back to Judea. He was fully aware that the Jews would once again try to stone him to death. When the disciples pointed this out, Jesus asked, "Are there not twelve hours in a day?" With this seemingly self-evident remark, Jesus wanted to convey that nothing happens before God's appointed time. As long as God granted Jesus daylight, he would be safe.

Then Jesus said, "Anyone who walks by day does not stumble but sees by the light of this world. Anyone who does not have this light and walks by night stumbles." He would grant safety to his disciples as they walked in the light of his presence. The time for Jesus' departure was at hand, and anyone who lacked his spiritual light would grope around in darkness.

Then Jesus clarified himself. He told the twelve disciples that their friend Lazarus had fallen asleep and that he would be going to Bethany to wake him up.

The disciples were ready to acknowledge that sound sleep would restore the physical health of Lazarus. But they pointed out that if his health would improve by sleep, there would be no need to travel toward Jerusalem. They could safely stay east of the Jordan and avoid an attack on Jesus and themselves.

Then Jesus told them that Lazarus had died and that he was glad not to have been in Bethany so that they might believe. Although this enigmatic remark failed to boost their confidence, the disciples sensed that an exceptional event would soon take place. Nevertheless, they remained apprehensive about their safety in Judea.

Thomas, known as the twin, courageously exhorted his fellow disciples to accompany Jesus to Judea and, if need be, to die with him there. This Thomas, who became known as a doubter, demonstrated unflinching courage, devotion, and a readiness to lay down his life for his teacher. His remark ought not to be understood as a willingness to die the death Jesus died. He uttered a call to all Christ's followers: "Be willing to die for your Master."

When Jesus and his band of twelve disciples arrived in Bethany, Lazarus had been buried four days. Burial in Israel normally occurred on the day of death because of the warm climate. By the fourth day, decomposition of the body would have set in, so that all hope of revival or resurrection would have ended. To be sure, the Jewish mourners could say that Jesus had come too late to raise him from the dead.

The smell of death not only hung over the body of Lazarus but drifted out of the tomb toward those who came near it.

The Tears of Jesus

Martha was the first to hear that Jesus had arrived. She was the older of the sisters and the leading figure in the family. Overcome by grief, Mary remained in the house, where she was comforted by relatives, friends, and acquaintances. But Martha rushed from the house to meet Jesus outside the village and informed him of what had happened in his absence.

All kinds of questions filled Martha's mind. Had Jesus not understood the severity of Lazarus's illness? Why had he delayed his coming? Did he not love them enough to come directly when he was called? She formulated a remark that could be taken as an accusation but actually was a word of regret: "Lord, if you had been here, my brother would not have died." Even so, Martha expressed her unshaken faith in Jesus and said, "However, I know even now that God will grant you whatever you ask him." Her remark could be called a faith that moves mountains.

Jesus lovingly comforted Martha with his assurance that Lazarus would rise again. Martha took his remark as a reference to the day of the resurrection at the end of time: "I know that at the last day in the resurrection, he will rise again." She articulated a confidence that came from her knowledge that at the end of the age the dead will arise from their graves.

Jesus then said to Martha, "I am the resurrection and the life." This amazing statement means that he has the power and the authority to raise his followers from the dead. He asked Martha if she believed this. Her reply was a confession of her genuine faith in him: "Yes, Lord, I believe that you are the Christ, the Son of God, who is the one coming into the world." Jesus stood next to Martha outside the village, and together they mourned the death of Lazarus. But Jesus wanted to speak to Mary too, and therefore he instructed Martha to call her sister.

Martha went back to the house, beckoned Mary away from the mourners, and told her privately, "The Teacher is here and is calling you." Instead of referring to Jesus by name, she used the word *Teacher* to indicate that Jesus had been teaching her.

Why would Jesus want to have Mary come to him outside the village? Certainly Jesus was not afraid of being arrested by the Jews, because he knew that his time had not yet come. Also, there is no indication that he wanted to be alone with Mary. The Jews, noticing that Mary had left the house, followed her. Jesus wanted both Mary and Martha to be outside the village near the cemetery to observe the miracle of the resurrection. And he also wanted the Jews to be witnesses of God's power.

When Mary got up and went to the place where Jesus was, she saw him and fell at his feet, overcome by her emotions. Of the two sisters, Mary was the one who could not control her emotions. She voiced the same words Martha had spoken to Jesus earlier: "Lord, if you had been here, my brother would not have died." Throughout the four days since the death of Lazarus, the sisters had repeated these words at home, and now in the presence of Jesus, they uttered them again.

When Jesus observed Mary weeping at his feet and heard the sobbing of the Jews, he became angry in spirit because of the ravages that sin and death had brought into this world, causing untold grief. Death had entered the family circle of his friends and caused him to be deeply moved and upset.

Jesus asked Mary and Martha where they had buried Lazarus. And they responded, "Come and see, Lord." Revealing that he was fully human, he shed tears. "Jesus wept." True, we could say that Jesus wept to express his sympathy for and love of the bereaved sisters, but on a deeper level, we know that his tears welled up because of the rage within him against the destructive power of death.

The Jews saw the tear-drenched face of Jesus and said, "See how much he loved Lazarus." Others questioned him, "Could not this one who opened the eyes of the blind man have prevented the death of Lazarus?" They did not use Jesus' name but referred to him as "this one," which may have been a cultural form of referring to a person. They expressed no ill will toward him, only approval of his love for Lazarus, but they based their remark on external observation. They were unable to understand the turmoil in Jesus' soul.

The Miracle of the Resurrection

Jesus was deeply moved in spirit because for him the moment had come to confront the power of death. Near the cemetery, he walked toward a cave that within it had a rock-hewn tomb covered with a stone. He instructed the bystanders to remove the stone, much to the consternation of Martha. She reminded Jesus that Lazarus had been dead for four days and that a bad odor emitted from his grave.

Even though fragrant spices had been placed around the body to minimize the smell of decomposition, it pervaded the entire area.

Jesus asked Martha, "Did I not tell you that if you believe, you will see the glory of God?" She had to admit that Jesus had said this to her and that she had expressed unwavering faith in him. She should have thought of Jesus' authority over death and should have looked forward to seeing God's glory displayed. The greatest miracle that Jesus had performed thus far in his ministry was about to happen, namely, the resurrection of a decomposing body.

After willing hands took away the stone and the stench became unbearable, Jesus offered a prayer to his Father in heaven. Jewish mourners were standing near the grave, and they were the people who needed to hear the prayer Jesus offered to his Father. He looked up to heaven and prayed, "Father, I thank you that you have heard me, and I know that you always hear me. But I said this on account of the crowd that is standing around me, that they may know that you have sent me."

This is a significant prayer. Jesus, addressing his Father, did not say "our Father," because his hearers had to understand the special relationship that exists between the Father and the Son. Also, the Jews had to hear and consequently acknowledge that Jesus indeed is the Son of God. He thanked his Father for having heard the prayer he had prayed privately concerning the raising of Lazarus.

Then in a loud voice he cried, "Lazarus, come out!" The volume of his voice was not meant for Lazarus. Jesus cried loudly so that all the bystanders could hear him and would sense that he spoke with the voice of divine authority. When Jesus spoke, the miracle of bringing together all the molecules in Lazarus's body was in a sense similar to God's speaking at creation. In Bethany re-creation took place in a split second, so that even the offensive smell of death vanished instantly.

Lazarus heard Jesus' command and stumbled out of the cave, bound hand and foot with burial bandages. Lazarus left the linen cloth behind but still had strips of cloth around his arms and legs and a sweatband around his head. Jesus instructed the bystanders to loosen the bands and to let him go home. Lazarus needed clothes and was not interested in answering questions about the life hereafter.

The effect of Lazarus's resurrection was mixed. It strengthened the faith of Mary and Martha as they rejoiced in having their family circle restored. Many of the Jews who witnessed the resurrection believed in Jesus. They could testify to others that Jesus was indeed the Messiah, the Son of the living God. Others reported the miracle to the Pharisees and hardened their unbelieving hearts.

After Lazarus was raised to life, he told everyone about Jesus Christ and his divine power to raise the dead. Many leading Jews believed this message, but others were filled with hatred toward Jesus. When these people saw that the crowds were following Jesus and putting their faith in him, they plotted to kill not only Jesus but also Lazarus. They considered Lazarus a witness who spread the teachings of the prophet of Nazareth. In their opinion, both the perpetrator of these teachings and his accomplice must die.

Application

The promise Martha received from Jesus holds true for everyone: "Anyone who believes in me will live, even though he or she dies a physical death; and all who live and believe in me will never die." This means that physical death is not final. After death, our spiritual life continues uninterrupted. When Jesus returns, soul and body will be reunited forever in glory.

Only Christianity teaches Jesus' resurrection. All other religions reject the belief that he rose from the grave and grants his followers the gift of eternal life. Members of other religions emphatically deny that Jesus has power over the grave and raises people from the dead. In their opinion, Jesus' triumph over death and the grave is an utterly preposterous doctrine. To them, death marks the end of physical life.

We who are Jesus' adherents candidly confess that by true faith we appropriate his resurrection and through him receive new life in body and soul.

Hence, we joyfully recite the Apostles' Creed, "I believe in the resurrection of the body."

People Who Became Jesus' Apostles

ANDREW

JOHN 1

From the House of a Fisherman

Jesus calls the seed of a mustard plant the smallest of all seeds. The plant grows in Palestine, and its seed is nothing more than a black speck. Once you drop that tiny seed onto the ground, you are unable to find it again. And yet when it germinates and the first leaves form, this little seedling eventually becomes a tree in whose branches the birds perch. With this illustration, Jesus depicted the growth of the Christian church, which began with the first disciple, Andrew.

Andrew was the brother of Simon Peter. He was born and raised in the Galilean village of Bethsaida, along the northern shore of the lake on the east bank of the Jordan, where he became a fisherman. The word *Bethsaida* in Hebrew signifies "house of the fisherman."

John the Baptist drew large crowds to the Jordan River near Jericho. Andrew, Simon Peter, Philip, John of Zebedee, and Nathanael—all from Galilee—left and traveled some sixty-five miles south along the Jordan to listen to this man, who in appearance and voice resembled the prophet Elijah of old.

They came to the place where John the Baptist was preaching a doctrine of repentance, telling the crowd that the kingdom of heaven was near. The people responded to his message, confessed their sins, and repented. Consequently, John baptized them.

One day Jesus appeared in the crowd while John was preaching. John, pointing to him, said, "Look, the Lamb of God that takes away the sin of the world!" A day later, John the Baptist once more said, but now especially to two of his disciples, "Look, the Lamb of God!"

Andrew and John of Zebedee left and followed Jesus. They spent the greater part of a day with him and became his disciples. During that day, they learned that Jesus indeed was the Messiah promised by God through the prophets.

After this first encounter with Jesus, Andrew enthusiastically went to his brother, Simon, and told him, "We have found the Messiah." He brought his brother to Jesus, who gave Simon a second name by calling him Cephas, which, translated from the Aramaic into Greek, means Peter. Subsequent to that first meeting, Andrew and the others went back to Galilee and took up their daily routine of fishing.

Jesus' second call to Andrew to be his disciple came when Andrew and Simon Peter were casting their net into the Lake of Galilee. He told the two brothers to follow him, for he would make them fishers of men. They left their fishing boats and nets and went along with Jesus.

Becoming a Follower of Jesus

How did Andrew interact with Jesus after he became his disciple? The gospel writers describe this in three instances. The first was on a Sabbath morning when Jesus preached in the Capernaum synagogue. After the worship service, Simon Peter and Andrew invited him to come to their home to heal Peter's mother-in-law, who was in bed, stricken by a high fever. Jesus took the woman's hand and healed her. She got up and immediately started to prepare the Sabbath meal for them.

On another occasion a crowd of thousands of people had come
to listen to Jesus preach. Near the end of the day, his disciples
asked him to send the crowd away so that they might go to the
neighboring villages to buy food. Jesus suggested that they feed
this multitude, but the disciples pointed out their lack of resources.
Then Jesus asked how much bread they had, and Andrew replied
that there was a little boy with five cakes of barley bread and two
small fish. He told Jesus that this insignificant quantity would never
feed a multitude. Jesus instructed his disciples to tell the crowd to
sit down on the green grass. The people sat in groups of hundreds
and fifties. After that Jesus looked up to heaven, gave thanks to God,
broke the bread, and multiplied the bread and the fish. The disciples
distributed the food to a crowd of five thousand, not counting the
women and children.

The last time we see Andrew interact with Jesus happens about
a week before Jesus' arrest and death on the cross. At that time,
crowds of worshipers traveled to Jerusalem for the annual Passover
Feast. There were some Greeks among them who also went to the
temple to worship God. They approached Philip, whose Greek
name suggests that he might have been able to converse in the
Greek language. The Greeks said to him, "Sir, we would like to see
Jesus." They were asking Philip for an interview with the Master.
Philip consulted with Andrew, and together they approached Jesus
with the request of these foreign worshipers.

Did these two disciples hesitate because these people, though
they went to Jerusalem to worship, were not Jews? If so, the possibility was real that the Greeks would interpret their hesitation as
an insult; they were God-fearers who worshiped at the temple in
the Court of the Gentiles. Philip and Andrew were in a quandary,
and all they could do was to acquaint Jesus with the request of
these Greeks.

We would have expected Jesus to welcome these Gentile visitors
and indicate that the gospel has a universal appeal to all nations and
peoples. But he did not respond to their request, for his reply was
directed to the event itself, namely, the hostile opposition of the
Jews versus the inquiry of the Gentiles. The Jewish leaders rejected
him, while a few outsiders were drawn to him.

Jesus said, "The hour has come for the Son of Man to be glorified." With these words, he informed the Greeks that the supreme hour of his passing from life to death was at hand. He was not interested in talking about earthly matters, for they had to receive him as their spiritual Messiah, by whose death and resurrection they would receive forgiveness of sins and eternal life.

Andrew was one of the disciples who, in bringing Greeks to Jesus, served him as a faithful representative. Whether these Gentiles understood Jesus' reply to their request is not known. In his Gospel, John relates that Jesus kept on teaching and performing miracles in Jerusalem until two days before the celebration of the Passover Feast. And John reports that many believed in Jesus.

Application

Andrew served as an intermediary who led others to Jesus. He brought his brother, Peter, to Jesus, the Christ. And again Andrew, with the help of Philip, introduced God-fearing Greeks to Jesus.

In a sense, all believers have been given the task to introduce others to the Lord Jesus Christ, who is the Light of the World. When God gives us opportunities to witness for him and to lead people to Christ, we should ask him to provide us with the right approach and fitting words. Then, led by the Spirit of God, we will be able to give our listeners the opportunity to see Jesus.

Ναθαναελ

A Person of Integrity

Parents who are contemplating what to name their newborn have numerous choices. Some people decide on a family name to continue their lineage. Others name their child after an influential person or use Bible names. A biblical name relates a message; for instance, Daniel means "God is my judge," Abigail denotes "father's joy," and Nathanael signifies "gift of God."

One of Jesus' first disciples was Nathanael, who was also known as Bartholomew, a surname that means "Son of Tholmai." He was born and raised in the Galilean town of Cana, where Jesus turned water into wine at a wedding celebration.

With Andrew, Peter, John of Zebedee, and Philip, Nathanael traveled south to a place along the Jordan where John the Baptist was preaching and baptizing people. He wanted to hear this Judean preacher. The question in their minds was whether John the Baptist was the promised Messiah, though John had emphatically denied

117

that he was the Christ by saying that he was not even worthy to
untie the thongs of the Messiah's sandals.

Both Andrew and John of Zebedee became Jesus' disciples, and
in quick succession Simon Peter, Philip, and Nathanael were added
to the group. Philip told Nathanael that Jesus of Nazareth, the son
of Joseph, was indeed the Messiah.

Nathanael was an outspoken person who did not hesitate to be-
little the town of Nazareth. He asked a negative rhetorical question:
"Can anything good come out of Nazareth?" The two towns Cana
and Nazareth were approximately three to four miles away from
one another and probably were rivals. Nathanael possibly knew
some of the people of Nazareth, a town with a mixed population of
Jews and Gentiles. It was a place where not only the religious level
of some people was low but also violence was not uncommon.

In short, the people of Nazareth were given a low rating by the
rest of the Galileans. Holding Nazareth in contempt, the Galileans
asked a number of questions based on the Scriptures:

- Could the Messiah come from Nazareth?
- Did not the prophet Micah predict that the Messiah would
  be born in Bethlehem of Judah?
- Wasn't the Messiah to come forth out of David's line, as the
  Scriptures predicted?

Consequently, Nathanael's question was direct, honest, and to the
point.

Philip's response was brief: "Come and see." He did not argue
with Nathanael but simply pointed him to Jesus, who had heard
every word.

Jesus was not offended but instead paid Nathanael a compliment.
He said, "Surely here is an Israelite in whom there is no deceit." No
better word could be spoken in praise of anyone. This does not mean
that Nathanael was perfect; rather Jesus read Nathanael's personality like an open book and saw nothing but honesty and integrity in
him. He was a man devoid of any trickery. Nathanael, the Israelite,
had a heart of gold and an upright spirit.

A Touching Confession

Nathanael was amazed. He said, "How do you know me?" This could be taken to mean that Jesus had often traveled to the village of Cana because of its proximity to Nazareth and that he had come to know a number of people living there. But it is better to say that Jesus, because of his divinity, saw what was in Nathanael.

Jesus answered, "Before Philip called you, when you were under the fig tree, I saw you." He made it known to him that nothing can be hidden from his sight and from his hearing. Even his negative question about Nazareth could not be kept from Jesus, but Jesus ignored it to focus attention on the Messiah. He revealed himself as the one who had divine insight. Jesus' remark about the fig tree immediately would prompt Nathanael to think of the Old Testament prophecies that revealed aspects of the coming kingdom of the Messiah. This kingdom would feature

- peace and security,
- the absence of fear,
- the epitome of love and obedience, and
- a reliance on God.

In that kingdom everyone would sit under his vine and under his own fig tree. With a reference to the fig tree, Jesus compelled Nathanael to look at the king in that kingdom, namely, the Messiah.

Nathanael responded to Jesus' fig-tree reference by acknowledging him as king. Thus he said, "Rabbi, you are the Son of God, you are the King of Israel." He had a change of heart and realized that in the presence of the Messiah, he had to address Jesus as Rabbi, that is, "my great Teacher."

He knew from the prophets that the Messiah would be the Son of God, and he realized that Jesus had proved his divinity. Also, Nathanael knew from the Psalms that the Son has an exclusive relationship with the Father.

Jesus asked Nathanael an additional question, though he did not expect an answer: "Because I said to you that I saw you under the fig tree, do you believe?" It was obvious that Nathanael had put his faith in Jesus, even though his faith was only in the beginning stages and had not stood the test of time. Nevertheless, Jesus had won a disciple who would follow him and do his bidding.

He gave Nathanael this promise: "Greater things than these you will see." This disciple stood at the threshold of his schooling, but by following his master, he would see the miracles of people raised from the dead, lepers restored, demon-possessed people set free, and the sick made well.

Jesus had still more to say to Nathanael: "Truly, truly, I say to you, you will see heaven opened and the angels of God ascending and descending upon the Son of Man." This was a direct reference to the dream Jacob had had after he fled from his brother, Esau. During the first night away from home, Jacob dreamed of a ladder that reached up to the throne of God in heaven, and he saw angels ascending and descending on it. Now Jesus prophesied that Nathanael would see that same ladder with angels going up and down and with Jesus as mediator between heaven and earth.

However, Jesus referred to himself not as the Son of God, as Nathanael confessed him to be, but as the Son of Man. Nathanael knew from the Scriptures that in the prophecy of Daniel, a person identified as the Son of Man came into the presence of the Almighty. This Son of Man took his place as the ruler over the whole earth and as king over a never-ending kingdom that could not be destroyed. To be the mediator between God and his people, Jesus had to be both human and divine. Accordingly, he used the title Son of Man.

Application

God looks at the heart, while we look at the face of a person. God told Samuel to anoint one of Jesse's sons to be king. Samuel observed only the outward appearance of David's brothers. But God looked at the heart and chose David. Similarly, Jesus looked at Nathanael and saw a heart of gold and an upright spirit.

Jesus has called you to be his disciple. He is the teacher and you are his student. He wants you to follow him and walk in his footsteps.

We often run ahead of ourselves in our desire to do something for Jesus. Not we but Jesus gives directives. He wants us to listen to his voice and expects us to be obedient to him. It is not what we do for the Lord that matters but what he wants us to do for him. He is our commander in chief.

PHILIP

Hesitant Philip

Philip was born and raised in a little fishing village called Bethsaida on the northeast shore of the Lake of Galilee. Jesus had performed a number of miracles in that village, but he had denounced the people, together with the neighboring village of Korazin, for their unrepentant attitude.

Philip, however, became a disciple of Jesus at the beginning of Jesus' ministry. And he became instrumental in directing Nathanael to Jesus.

The Gospel of John mentions Philip only incidentally. For example, when Jesus had been preaching to the crowd of five thousand and the disciples asked Jesus to send the people away so they could buy food in the neighboring villages, Jesus turned to Philip and asked, "Where shall we buy bread for these people to eat?"

Philip knew the area well because it was relatively close to Bethsaida. He realized that the multitude would be unable to find sufficient bread in a few local bakeries. Philip responded, "Two hundred denarii [a day-laborer's wages for eight months of work] would be insufficient to buy bread so that everyone might have something to eat." He had quickly estimated what was needed to feed this crowd of people.

When Andrew brought the boy with five small barley loaves and two small fish to Jesus, he too pointed out the utter inadequacy of the available food. It would take a miracle to feed this multitude. Then in the presence of his disciples and the crowd, Jesus multiplied the loaves and fishes so that everyone had enough to eat.

At another time, some Greeks approached Philip as they were traveling to Jerusalem with Jewish pilgrims to celebrate the Passover Feast. They were Gentiles who spoke Greek and had become either God-fearers or converts to Judaism. Perhaps because Philip had a Greek name, they approached him and said, "Sir, we would like to see Jesus."

They had heard about Jesus of Nazareth, who preached the Good News of forgiveness of sin and life eternal. Would Jesus welcome Gentiles into the fellowship of his adherents? The problem became too big for Philip, and cautious by nature, he did not want to act alone. Thus, he went to Andrew and informed him of the Greeks' request. Together they went to Jesus and introduced them to him.

Jesus answered their request by saying that the hour had come for the Son of Man to be glorified. This would happen much the same way as a grain of wheat falls to earth and dies to give birth to a plant that bears much fruit. Jesus would die but come to life again to bring forth an abundant spiritual harvest that would include both Jewish and Gentile converts.

A few days later, Jesus celebrated the Passover Feast with his disciples in Jerusalem. After he instituted the Lord's Supper, he delivered his farewell discourse, in which he told them that he would return to his Father in heaven, where he would prepare a place for them. He said, "I am the way and the truth and the life. No one comes to the Father except through me. If you have come to know me, you will also know my Father. From now on, you do know him and have seen him."

To know Jesus is to know the Father, and to see Jesus is to see the Father. Jesus is the Father's representative and speaks the very words of God.

This information was too complicated for Philip, whose mind could not comprehend that the Father and the Son are one in essence. He with his fellow disciples had come to know Jesus as teacher, miracle-worker, Son of God, and Messiah. He had acknowledged the divinity and humanity of Jesus, but knowing and seeing Jesus as the Father's identity was too much for him.

Having seen Jesus' glory, Philip now asked, "Lord, show us the Father and it will satisfy us." On Mount Sinai, Moses had wanted God to show him his glory, but all he was permitted to view was the back of God. People in Old Testament days believed that to see God's face would cause death. But Philip was not asking Jesus to reveal God's face; rather, he wanted him to show evidence of the Father's glory.

Jesus replied, "Have I been with you for such a long time, and yet you have not come to know me, Philip?" For three years, Jesus had taught his disciples the truths of God's kingdom and had revealed the Father in his person and actions. They knew him as the Son, who functioned as mediator between the Father and God's people.

Jesus said that if Philip had paid attention and had reflected on his words and deeds, he would have recognized the Father in him. Jesus asked, "How can you say, 'Show us the Father'?"

In a clear statement, Jesus taught Philip the unity of the Father and the Son by telling him that the one is in the other and that the two are one in essence. Although this is a mystery that the human mind will never be able to fathom, Jesus made this teaching clear by asking Philip, "Do you not believe that I am in the Father and the Father is in me?" And Philip had to say yes.

Jesus taught Philip and the rest of the disciples that he differed markedly from the prophets, who had to introduce their prophecies with the phrase, "This is what the Lord says." Jesus, because of his unity with the Father, spoke on his own authority. All his words came from the Father, yet they were genuinely his own. Also, whatever Jesus did was in harmony with the will of the Father and came from the Father.

Application

Christians face a mystery in trying to explain the relationship of Jesus' humanity to his divinity. We face other mysteries as well:

Human authors wrote the Bible, yet God inspired the Holy Scriptures. Jesus was born into the human race, yet as the Son of God he is divine. And Paul tells us to work out our salvation with fear and trembling, yet it is God who redeems us. These mysteries will always perplex us. Nevertheless, we know that God will grant us insight in the world to come.

How do you explain these mysteries to those who wish to see Jesus? The answer is that we worship a personal God and accept in faith everything he has revealed to us in his Son. What is beyond our human understanding belongs to God, but what is revealed to us and can be known belongs to us.

Thomas

The Daring of Doubting Thomas

Doubt is the opposite of faith and frequently plagues the follower of Christ. The word *doubt* derives from the term *duo*. It implies that there are two different paths we can follow: the one is right, the other wrong. If someone calls you a doubting Thomas, it is not a flattering remark.

Who was Thomas? He was called Didymus, which means "twin," although we will never know whose twin he was. In the lists of the Twelve, Thomas is paired with Matthew and with Philip, but we don't know whether this is meaningful. We have no further information about his place of residence but assume that he was born and raised in Galilee. There is some evidence that he may have been known as Judas Thomas.

The byword *doubting Thomas* identifies him. When Mary and Martha sent word to Jesus from Bethany that their brother, Lazarus, was ill and probably would die, Jesus remained on the other side of the

126

Jordan for another two days. One of the reasons Jesus stayed away was the threat to his life.

When Jesus made it known that he would go to Bethany, the disciples tried to dissuade him, reminding him that the Jewish authorities in Jerusalem wanted to stone him. They thought it would not be safe for Jesus to travel to the vicinity of the capital. Jesus, however, taught them that nothing happens by chance and that he was not walking by night but in the light. He said that he was going to Bethany to wake up Lazarus, who had fallen asleep. He was speaking figuratively, for Lazarus had died and Jesus would go there to bring him back to life.

Thomas understood the necessity of going to Lazarus, and he showed his courage to the rest of the disciples by being willing to accompany Jesus even in the face of death. He was an example of devoted loyalty to his Master. Yet at the same time, his words betrayed a touch of fatalism. He said to his fellow disciples, "Let us also go that we may die with Jesus." He did not mean that he would die the same death Jesus died, but he demonstrated his willingness to give up his life for him.

Thomas had an uncomplicated personality that exhibited honesty and integrity. This became evident when Jesus informed his disciples that he was going to his Father's house, which has many rooms. He would go there to prepare a place for them so that they too might be where he would be. And he added that they knew the way to the place where he was going.

Revealing ignorance and a measure of simplicity, Thomas said, "Lord, we do not know where you are going. How can we know the way?" He verbalized what the others were thinking. But no words of reproof came from Jesus' lips, only words of further instruction.

Jesus answered, "I am the way, and the truth, and the life. No one comes to the Father except through me." He did not indicate how to find the way but stated unequivocally that he himself is the way. He meant that his way leads to God the Father, for Jesus is the mediator between God and humanity. When he stated that he is the way, he specified that there is no other way to come to God than through his Son, Jesus Christ. Further, Jesus said, "I am the truth," and thus he personifies truth. And Jesus said that he is the life, which means that he is the source of life eternal. Thomas and the rest of the disciples could not have received a clearer word from Jesus about the exclusive way to come to God the Father.

Doubting Gives Birth to Faith

On Easter Sunday, Jesus appeared to the women, Mary Magdalene, the two people from Emmaus, Peter, and the ten disciples in the Upper Room. But Thomas was not with them on any of these occasions. He stayed away from his fellow disciples and friends, and when he met them, he expressed his sincere doubts about Jesus' resurrection. He told them that unless he saw the marks in Jesus' hands and touched his side, he refused to believe.

Even though Jesus had repeatedly taught his disciples that he would be killed but that on the third day he would rise from the dead, Thomas rejected all the evidence that had been presented to him. For him, Jesus had died a horrible death on the cross and was buried in a tomb outside Jerusalem. Thomas would have to meet the resurrected Jesus, see and touch the marks on his body, before he could accept the reality of the living Christ.

Thomas remained unconvinced no matter who talked to him about meeting Jesus. But exactly a week after Jesus' resurrection, Thomas was with the other ten disciples in the Upper Room, with the doors locked for safety. Suddenly Jesus stood in their midst and said, "Peace be with you," which is a common greeting in Hebrew even today.

Jesus came a second time in as many weeks, this time to single out Thomas. He was thoroughly acquainted with Thomas's objections. Now Jesus spoke the very words of Thomas and told him to put his finger in the nail marks on his hands and to bring his hand to Jesus' side. Then he helped Thomas out of his unbelief by admonishing him to believe.

Instead of rebuking Thomas for his stubborn refusal to believe, Jesus lovingly persuaded him to accept the reality of his resurrection. Thomas uttered the words, "My Lord and my God." No other words could describe Thomas's transformation; he confessed that Jesus was not only his Lord but also his God. He now fully understood Jesus' teaching of the unity of Father and Son; that is, as the Father is divine, so is the Son.

Jesus responded to his confession by reaffirming Thomas: "Because you have seen me, you have believed." And then he added this beatitude for future generations: "Blessed are they who have not seen and yet have believed." He did not mean to say that those who have seen and believe are placed at a lower level than those who have not seen and believe. Rather, Jesus communicated to Thomas that he was highly privileged to have seen Jesus in the flesh raised from the dead. All others who did not have that advantage would have to rely on reading and hearing about Jesus' resurrection and then come to faith in him.

Application

The love of the Lord Jesus Christ overwhelms us. We notice that he did not rebuke Thomas but tenderly told him to place his finger on the nail marks of his hands and to put his hand on the spear mark in his side. Then he looked him in the eye and said, "Stop doubting and believe." Jesus encourages us to look to him, the author and perfecter of our faith, for in him we are victorious and overcome our doubts and fears.

Jesus has boundless patience with us when we express doubts and misgivings. He stands next to us and always strengthens us, so that we may become heroes of faith.

PETER THE FISHERMAN

The Catch of Their Lives

Simon, known as Son of John, was born and raised in Bethsaida, a village on the east bank of the Jordan River along the north shore of the Lake of Galilee. He and his brother, Andrew, were fishermen, as was their father.

When he came of age, Simon married and took up residence in the town of Capernaum, which is on the northwestern shore of the Lake of Galilee. He at one time accompanied some men from Capernaum south along the Jordan to a place where John the Baptist was preaching a message of repentance and baptizing those who repented of their sins.

There he met Jesus of Nazareth, who had given him the name Peter, which means "rock." Although he and Andrew then became disciples of Jesus, they returned home to Capernaum and continued their fishing trade.

On one occasion, Peter and Andrew had been fishing at all hours of the night with their partners, James and John. When morning broke, they had caught not even a single fish and came to shore with empty boats. There they were washing and mending their nets in preparation for the following night.

Then Jesus approached Peter and told him to go out into the deep water and let down his net for a catch of fish. This request was too much for Peter. He knew that Jesus was a carpenter from Nazareth. What would a carpenter know about catching fish? No expert fisherman would waste his time trying to make a catch in the middle of the day. But if Jesus insisted, Peter would oblige and prove him wrong.

As soon as Peter and Andrew had cast their nets into the water, they realized that they would have success. When they began to haul the nets aboard, the number of fish was so large that the nets began to break. They quickly signaled James and John, who were standing on shore, to come with their boat and help them garner the catch.

Both boats soon were filled to overflowing, and the weight of the fish nearly caused them to sink. By all standards, this catch was miraculous. They would need extra hands to empty the boats and process the fish for market. The income this catch would bring these fishermen would be extraordinary. With this supernatural gift from God, they could support their families for the immediate future.

A New Kind of Fishing

Although Jesus recently had given Peter the new name Rock, this disciple certainly had not demonstrated a rock-like faith in Christ. His comment was marked by skepticism: "Master, all night long we have toiled and caught nothing, but because you say so, I'll let down the nets." And now these words haunted him, for he had been a man not of faith but of doubt.

Simon Peter realized that Jesus was no ordinary human being but one who possessed divine power. When Peter with his companions saw all the fish, he was overwhelmed in the presence of Jesus and fell down on his knees in a worshipful posture. He exclaimed, "Go away from me, Lord; I am a sinful man." The contrast of a sinful, doubting fisherman with a holy and sinless Jesus was too great for

Peter, who was struck with awe and reverential fear. He and his
fellow fishermen now understood that the carpenter of Nazareth
was divine, the Son of God, the Messiah.

In the sacred presence of the divine Jesus, sinful Peter experienced trepidation. He understood that Jesus was in full control and
ruled even the fish in the Lake of Galilee. Not Peter but Jesus knew
everything about the fishing trade.

Jesus spoke no words of rebuke and did not depart. On the contrary, he told Peter not to be afraid. He spoke the language of fishermen when he told him, "From now on I'll make you fish for people."
That was the dramatic turning point in Peter's life, for it meant that
he would leave his occupation as fisherman and become a full-time
disciple of Jesus. Not only Peter but also his companions, Andrew,
James, and John, left their boats, nets, families, and sources of income
to follow Jesus.

Why did Jesus tell these men that they would be fishing for
people? Would it not have been better if he had called them to be
shepherds of sheep or sowers of seed? The term *shepherd* conjures up
the image of a person who devotes tender loving care to the rams,
ewes, and lambs of his flock. In the same way, a pastor is called a
shepherd when he cares for the members of his congregation. A
shepherd can predict with a high degree of certainty the increase
of his flock when in springtime the lambs are born. He can rely on
this increase for his annual income.

Jesus could have used the term *sowers of the Word*, for God's servants
go forth on the Lord's Day expounding the Scriptures week after
week. And again, someone who sows grain at planting time can
be reasonably assured of a harvest. The size of the crop may vary
depending on weather conditions, diseases, and the effectiveness of
fertilizers and pesticides, but farmers always reap a crop.

Fishermen are not always sure of a catch. When Jesus told Peter
and his companions, "I'll make you fish for people," he did not guar-
antee that they would have success. They would lack certainty, and
therefore they would have to depend entirely on God to bless their
labors. God would send them to teach the people the Scriptures and
to lead them to Christ. Their preaching, however, did not always
result in the founding of a church. Paul tried to bring Christ's gospel

to the people in Athens, but he had to leave that city without gaining a meaningful group of followers.

Jesus instructed his disciples on their first mission tour that they could expect opposition as they tried to evangelize the people. He told them that if a person or family did not receive them, they would have to shake the dust off their sandals and leave that home or town. Jesus was sending them forth like sheep among wolves. But those people who were amenable to hearing God's Word would receive the unique blessing of God's peace filling their homes.

Application

When a church sends forth missionaries, its members should sustain them financially and pledge their daily prayer support. Without dedicated prayer, the work of missionaries suffers and often fails. The forces of Satan's kingdom are strong and are determined to thwart the work of God. Preachers and missionaries should place their full trust in God, who sends them forth with the gospel of peace and makes them victorious in the Lord. He will give them tangible results.

The growth of the church is hampered most when people fail to pray for pastors, evangelists, missionaries, and teachers of the Word. In contrast, the church grows and develops only if God's people faithfully and consistently pray and work.

Peter the Leader

Top Dog

Almost from the beginning of his discipleship, Peter showed a natural talent for being a leader. The lists of the twelve disciples in the Gospels of Matthew, Mark, and Luke and in the Book of Acts always place Peter at the top. Even in the combination of the names Peter and Paul, Peter's name always comes first. His name appears more than any other disciple's in the four Gospels and Acts.

Jesus chose Peter and the brothers James and John to make up the inner circle of the twelve disciples. This inner circle was with Jesus at specific occasions when he displayed his divine power or origin. These three were asked to accompany Jesus into the bedroom of Jairus's twelve-year-old daughter, who lay dead. They were with him at the time of Jesus' transfiguration. And in the Garden of Gethsemane, Jesus asked them to watch and pray.

Peter did not hesitate to confess the identity of Jesus. Take, for example, the incident on the storm-tossed Lake of Galilee. After

Jesus had fed a multitude of five thousand people near the lake, he sent his disciples away in a boat while he stayed behind to pray.

The lake was stormy with high waves and a strong wind, and the disciples, having rowed all night, still had not been able to come ashore. Then they saw Jesus walking toward them on the waves. They were terrified. But coming near, Jesus told them to be courageous and not afraid.

Seeing Jesus standing on the water, Peter asked him if he too could stand on the water. When Jesus invited him to come, Peter stood and walked on the waves. But the moment he failed to look at Jesus, he sank into the water and cried, "Lord, save me!" Jesus took him by the hand, pulled him up, and rebuked him for his lack of faith. Peter and the disciples were overwhelmed by the power Jesus demonstrated over nature and worshiped him, saying, "Truly you are the Son of God."

Peter's Confession of Faith

At a later date, as Jesus traveled through northern Israel, he asked his disciples, "Who do the people say the Son of Man is?" Jesus always referred to himself as the Son of Man and never as the Son of God, because he knew that if he identified himself as the Son of God, the religious hierarchy would accuse him of blasphemy. He had performed numerous miracles, had preached in various synagogues, and had instructed large crowds of people. By means of these miracles he had demonstrated divine power. Now the time had come to ask his disciples whether the people realized who he was.

The answers the disciples gave Jesus included John the Baptist, Elijah, Jeremiah, and other prophets. According to the Old Testament prophet Malachi, Elijah would return as a forerunner of the Messiah. Malachi did not mean that Elijah would personally prepare the way for the Messiah. He used the name figuratively. Jeremiah was one of the major Old Testament prophets, whose return some people expected. But he had not yet returned.

Jesus then pointedly asked the disciples how they identified him: "But you, who do you say that I am?" They should have had the answer at the tips of their tongues, for they had called him the Son of God when Jesus pulled Peter out of the water on that stormy night. Simon Peter became their spokesman and said, "You are the Christ, the Son of the living God." This was Peter's finest hour.

Jesus responded by pointing to God the Father and said, "Blessed are you, Simon, son of John. Not flesh and blood but my Father in heaven has revealed this to you." As the spokesman for the disciples, Simon had now lived up to the name that Jesus had given him. Now he had shown his rock-like faith in Christ his Savior. Yet Jesus traced the confession itself back to God the Father, who had revealed it to Peter and his fellow disciples. He called Peter blessed, which means that God extended his favor to him so that divine bliss surrounded him.

After exalting Peter with this beatitude, Jesus granted him an additional blessing: "And I tell you, you are Peter, and on this rock I will build my church." Jesus was playing with words when he said it: "You are *Petros* [rock], and on this *Petra* [rock] I will build my church."

What did Jesus mean by this cryptic remark? If Jesus had wanted to indicate that the church would be built on Peter, he could have said, "You are Peter, and on you I will build my church." Instead he used the word *petra* to convey the idea that the rock-like confession of Peter's faith in Christ constitutes the church's foundation.

Jesus discerned in Peter's confession the boldness and firmness that are basic to the establishment of God's kingdom on this earth. He conveyed the thought that the rock is Peter, who expressed his unquestionable faith in Jesus. Whereas Jesus Christ is the foundation of the church, Peter and the other apostles serve as its substructure. This apostolic substructure is the rock on which the church is built, and Peter functions as the leader of the apostles.

Jesus told Peter that the gates of hell would not be able to overpower the church. The gates of hell figuratively means the powers of Satan that come forth out of hell and seek to eradicate the church. Jesus says that Satan is unable to destroy the church. He is given permission to kill the followers of Christ, but he learns that countless others take their places. Taking hold of the church is similar to taking hold of quicksilver with a bare hand; it scatters and rolls away into numerous places.

Application

Peter, as the representative and leader of the disciples, received the keys of the kingdom of heaven. Keys function as symbols of authority by which doors can be opened and shut. The keys are, first, the proclamation of the gospel and, second, the exclusion of anything that is contrary to Christ's teaching and conduct. The preaching of his gospel opens the way to God the Father, and the exercise of discipline results in the exclusion of everything that is offensive.

When the teaching of the Good News leads sinners to repentance and faith, the gateway to heaven is opened wide. But when people intentionally sin against God and his revealed Word, heaven remains closed.

Today is the day of grace in which God graciously makes his salvation known. Now is the time to choose life and not death.

PETER'S FAILURE

From Summit to Valley

Though he was called a man of faith, Peter had feet of clay and many times was the chief of failures. Immediately after he had spoken memorable words regarding Jesus' identity, he failed utterly in being an obedient disciple. Therefore he needed words of rebuke and correction. Because Peter reflects the spiritual inconsistencies in our lives, we see our mirror image in him and know that there is hope when Jesus rescues us.

The counterpart of a mountaintop experience is a deep valley of dismay. If Peter's confession, "You are the Christ, the Son of the living God," is the mountaintop, then his attempt to rebuke Jesus is the deep valley of disappointment. In the one experience, God the Father guided Peter, while in the other, Satan influenced him. Yet Jesus remained in full control of the situation and taught Peter and the other disciples what a follower of Jesus ought to do.

After Jesus acknowledged Peter's confession that he was the Christ, he told his disciples what the future had in store for him to fulfill his role as Messiah. He explained to them that he had to go to Jerusalem to suffer many things at the hands of the religious leaders.

138

These people would cause Jesus to suffer at his trial and then have him killed. Jesus taught his disciples that on the third day, he would rise from the dead.

The Twelve were shocked to hear Jesus speak about suffering and being killed. They were too stunned to understand his remark about rising from the grave. It would take repetitive teaching before the reality of Jesus' death and resurrection would set in and make sense to his disciples. When eventually they met the risen Christ, they would go forth as his apostles to proclaim the resurrection as the basis of the Christian faith.

But Peter rashly thought that it was his task to take Jesus aside for a word of admonition. Although he meant well, he placed himself above his teacher, as if Jesus needed a word of reproof from the lips of Peter. He started to rebuke Jesus by saying, "May God be merciful to you, Lord; this will never happen to you." Peter actually tried to convey to Jesus that his remarks about suffering and death were unacceptable.

Jesus heard the voice of Satan in Peter's admonition. Satan had taken him to a high mountain to show him all the kingdoms of the world and their glory. Then he said to Jesus, "I'll give all these to you, if only you will kneel down and worship me." In response, Jesus rebuked him and said, "Get out of here, Satan!"

Now facing Peter and the rest of his disciples, Jesus uttered the same words: "Get away from me, Satan!" He knew that Satan used the mind and mouth of Peter to try to dissuade Jesus from going to the cross to fulfill his messianic task. Though Jesus faced Peter, he addressed Satan and said, "You are tempting me to sin, because you have in mind human things and not the things of God."

If for one moment Jesus should have considered Peter's rebuke, he would have fallen into Satan's trap and could no longer be the Messiah. As a consequence, Peter would never have been set free from the curse of sin and guilt. In God's plan, Jesus had to go to the cross, suffer, die, and rise from the dead to redeem his people.

The time had come for Jesus to show the Twelve how they might be his disciples. They would have to deny themselves, take up their crosses, and follow him. Peter eventually learned that lesson and applied it in the service of his Lord. As an apostle, he followed in Jesus' footsteps and later, according to tradition, died on a cross upside down. He denied himself so that Jesus might receive the glory.

Threefold Denial

Peter had to learn the lesson of following Jesus the hard way. In response to Jesus' comment on the eve of his crucifixion that all of his disciples would fall away, Peter boldly stated that even if all would desert him, he would never do that. Then Jesus told him that during that very night, before the rooster crowed, he would disown Jesus three times. Again Peter opened his mouth and boldly declared, "Even if I have to die with you, I will never disown you." Peter was not alone, for all the other disciples affirmed the same thing. He would have done better if he had observed the rule, "Never say never unless you are absolutely sure." Twice in quick succession, he emphatically stated that he would never desert or disown Jesus.

When Jesus had instructed the Twelve how to be disciples, he said that they had to deny themselves, take up the crosses they had to bear, and follow him. Now Jesus repeated the same verb *to deny* and told Peter that before the rooster crowed to announce the approaching daybreak, Peter would deny him three times.

Disregarding Jesus' prediction, Peter vehemently stated that he would never deny him. In that same context, Peter heard Jesus say that he had prayed for him that his faith might not fail. Satan had asked God for permission to sift the Twelve as wheat.

Jesus extended pastoral care to Peter and even hinted at reinstating him after Peter had failed to acknowledge him three times. Jesus said that after he had turned around and acknowledged his sin, Peter should strengthen his brothers.

In the Garden of Gethsemane, Jesus asked Peter and the two sons of Zebedee to watch and pray. But the three fell asleep while Jesus prayed. When he came back to them, he berated them for their inability to stay awake for even one hour. He admonished them to watch and pray and not fall into temptation. When he came back a second and third time, he found them still asleep. He instructed them to get up, for the hour of his betrayal had come.

As the high priest, Caiaphas, interrogated Jesus, Peter entered the courtyard of the high priest and warmed himself at a fire that the servants and officials had lit on that chilly night. The servant girl who had admitted him said, "You are one of this man's disciples, aren't you? You also were with Jesus of Nazareth." But in the presence of all the servants and officials, Peter blurted out, "I don't know what you are talking about." He publicly declared that he had nothing to do with Jesus.

Peter walked away from there and went to the entryway, where another servant girl identified Peter as one of Jesus the Nazarene's disciples. Once more, Peter denied having any knowledge of the man, and he confirmed it with an oath. He called Jesus "the man" to indicate that he had never heard of him.

But Peter's speech betrayed him as a Galilean, so his bystanders remarked, "Certainly you are one of them, for your accent gives you away." He tried to defend himself by cursing himself and shouting, "I don't know the man!" Then suddenly a rooster crowed, as Jesus had predicted. Peter remembered his master's words: "Before the rooster crows, you will deny me three times."

In spite of Simon Peter's bold statements that he would defend Jesus come what may, he had repudiated his master three times in front of all the people in the high priest's courtyard. And yet Jesus opened the way for repentance by causing Peter to remember his warning. Simon went outside the gate, and there he wept bitterly, shedding tears of contrition and shame.

Peter had been a failure during the three years he followed Jesus. He lacked faith to walk with Jesus on the water of the Lake of Galilee. He rebuked Jesus for predicting his trial and death. He said he would defend Jesus and even die for him, but instead he fled and disowned him three times.

Application

Peter's denial of Jesus led to sincere repentance. Weeping bitterly, he returned to his fellow disciples. He admitted to them that he had denied Jesus. And his admission of guilt resulted in forgiveness and eventually to his reinstatement.

We can relate to Peter, for we too sin against Jesus and our fellow man. Though we wrap ourselves in guilty silence, we know full well that we must confess our sin. We are unable to look one another in the eye until we admit being wrong and ask the injured party to forgive us.

What a relief when sin is forgiven and relations are restored! The memory of our sin lingers, but the burden of guilt has been removed. We make a 180-degree turn by abandoning the sins of the past and dedicating our lives to the glory of God and the well-being of others.

PETER'S REINSTATEMENT

Not Home, Gone Fishing

After Jesus rose from the dead, he instructed his disciples to return to Galilee, where he would meet them and give them further instructions.

When the disciples arrived in Capernaum and Bethsaida, they went back to their former occupations. Peter took up fishing in the Lake of Galilee and invited his fellow disciples to go with him. Seven of them went. They were Simon Peter, Thomas, Nathanael, James and John, and two other disciples whose names are not mentioned.

Their return to their former occupation seemed to be a regression. Should they not have devoted their time to evangelizing the cities, towns, and villages in Galilee and Judea? Indeed, Jesus wanted to meet them in Galilee to send them forth as his apostles. But he would have to reinstate Peter before he could commission him as a spiritual shepherd and overseer of the church.

After fishing throughout the night without any result, the disciples headed for the beach. They saw a person standing on the shore but did not realize that the man was Jesus. He called out to them, "Friends, don't you have any fish?" They said, "No." Then he told them to cast their net on the right side of the boat and they would catch some fish. No one objected to the stranger's order. When they cast their net, they caught a large number of fish, filling the net to capacity. They were unable to take the fish into the boat and had to drag the net to shore.

As they were coming closer to shore and the morning fog began to dissipate, John recognized Jesus and alerted Peter. When Simon realized that the stranger was the Lord, he could not wait any longer to be near him. He put on his outer garment and held it in place with his belt. Then he jumped overboard, leaving the others to maneuver both net and boat to shore.

Peter swam straight to Jesus and saw that he had breakfast ready for them. Jesus had prepared a fire of burning coals on which he had placed a fish; also he had some bread. Jesus instructed his disciples to give him some of the fish they had just caught, so that he could serve them a full meal. Simon Peter went aboard the boat and helped the others to drag the net ashore. One of them started counting, and the catch came to 153 large fish. Then Jesus invited them to have breakfast.

Simon and the other disciples realized that Jesus was teaching them a repeat lesson not in catching fish but in catching people for his church and kingdom. At the outset of their discipleship, some of them had witnessed an extraordinary catch of fish. And Jesus had told them at that time, "From now on, you will be catching people instead of fish." That time the net tore, whereas this time it stayed intact. The net of Christ's gospel will take in countless people, and yet the net will not break.

None of the disciples dared to ask Jesus to identify himself, even though they knew he was the risen Christ. They were a little uncertain about how to relate to him. When he had met them on the first evening of his resurrection, they had given him a piece of broiled fish. He had eaten it to prove that he had a body of flesh and bones. Now once again, he ate with his disciples to indicate that though he had risen from the dead, his body was real.

Peter the Apostle

Simon Peter had personally met Jesus on Easter Sunday and again
that evening in the Upper Room, as well as a week later. He had
heard him say to the disciples who were present, "As the Father has
sent me, so send I you" (John 20:21).

But Peter's personal relationship to Jesus had to be restored. His
disowning of the Lord had never been resolved in the presence of
his fellow disciples. When he had refused to acknowledge Jesus
in the courtyard of the high priest, he had lost his right to be an
apostle. In this courtyard Peter had warmed himself at a charcoal
fire. Now on the beach of the Lake of Galilee, Jesus had prepared a
charcoal fire to broil fish. With these striking symbols, he proceeded
to reinstate Simon, asking him, "Simon, son of John, do you love
me more than these?"

The mood in this after-breakfast setting was solemn. Jesus singled
out Peter from among the seven disciples who were present and laid
before them the matter of Peter's penitence. He addressed Simon by
name as the others listened. Three times Jesus asked Peter the same
question, reminding him that three times he had disowned his Lord.

The first question Jesus posed was "Simon, son of John, do you
love me more than these?" Was Jesus asking whether Peter loved
Jesus more than the others loved him? Or did he want to know
whether Peter loved Jesus more than he loved the other disciples?
The answer is yes in both cases, but the first question takes priority in view of Peter's leadership position. Simon had placed himself
above the others when he had said, "Even if all desert you, I'll never
desert you." Now Jesus asked him if Peter showed a higher degree
of love for him than the other disciples did.

The moment of truth for Peter had come. His answer was brief,
but it came from his heart: "Yes, Lord, you know that I love you."
Jesus responded, "Feed my lambs." The switch from being a fisherman to a shepherd must be seen in the context of Jesus' statement,
"I am the good shepherd. The good shepherd lays down his life for
the sheep." The underlying message demanded from Peter the same
love as Jesus had shown through his death on the cross.

Earlier, Simon had solemnly declared, "Even if I have to die with you, I will never disown you." Jesus held him to his words and told him to feed the spiritual lambs in the church. He had to leave his boat and nets behind; Jesus called him to a full-time ministry in which he had to function as a pastor to the flock.

Then Jesus asked Peter a second time, "Simon, son of John, do you love me?" How heartrending this must have been for Simon to hear Jesus ask the very same question, with the omission of the comparative phrase *more than these*. This omission made the second question more personal. It would almost seem as if the Lord put little stock in the answer Peter had given him.

Would Peter indeed follow Jesus unwaveringly, even if it cost him his life in the ministry of the Word of God? Simon answered his Lord by uttering the same words he had used unwaveringly the first time: "Yes, Lord, you know that I love you." Again the words came from the bottom of his heart. Jesus gave him the charge, "Shepherd my sheep."

Once more, Jesus focused attention on the role he gave Peter as apostle. This charge Simon took to heart in his ministry. In one of his epistles, he instructed the elders to be shepherds of God's flock. And he added that when the Chief Shepherd appeared, they would receive a crown of unfading glory.

Then a third time Jesus asked, "Simon, son of John, do you love me?" Peter was grieved that Jesus would ask him three times whether he loved the Lord. Did Jesus doubt his commitment to love and serve him with all his heart, soul, and mind? He answered, "Lord, you know all things; you know that I love you."

Peter acknowledged that Jesus, in his divinity, knew all things. He confessed that Jesus was fully acquainted with his love for the Lord. Jesus then gave him the third charge, which combined the first two: "Feed my sheep." That is, he had to feed the members of the church spiritual food. If they should wander, he would have to bring them back to the fold and be their tenderly loving shepherd.

Thus, Jesus restored Peter to the office of apostle: "As the Father sent me, so send I you." Now he could be Jesus' ambassador, standing before thousands of Jews at Pentecost, preaching in Solomon's Colonnade, calling the members of the Sanhedrin to salvation in Jesus, and bringing Christ's gospel to the Gentiles in Caesarea. He truly was an undaunted servant of his Lord and Master, Jesus Christ.

Application

After Peter was reinstated, he revealed a latent talent to lead his fellow apostles and to take a leading role in the developing church in Jerusalem. He skillfully addressed the members of the Sanhedrin and boldly told them that to be saved, they had to believe in Jesus, for his name was the only one under heaven that led to salvation. Peter proved to be a model of courage, boldness, sagacity, and prudence.

Jesus gave his apostles the charge to be his witnesses from Jerusalem to the ends of the earth. And this divine command is valid for all Christians. Wherever the Lord has placed us in life, we must testify for him. This calls for audacity and good judgment on our part. Sometimes we must speak boldly for Christ. At other times our attitude and actions speak louder than words.

JOΗΠ

John's Distinctiveness

In countries around the world, the name John appears in numerous languages. Here are just a few: Ian, Ivan, Jean, Juan, Jan, and Johan.

The name John derives from the Hebrew *Johanan*, which signifies "to whom the LORD is gracious" or "whom the LORD has graciously given." It is a common name in the New Testament.

John's father was Zebedee; his mother was Salome, who was a sister of Jesus' mother, Mary, with the result that Jesus and John were cousins. This blood relationship became strikingly meaningful when Jesus, addressing both his mother and John from the cross, committed Mary into the care of her nephew.

Jesus gave James and John the name Boanerges (Sons of Thunder). This name fit their character, as exemplified by the incident when Jesus traveled with his disciples through Samaria on the way to Jerusalem. When they wished to spend the night in a certain village, the Samaritans did not welcome them. This rebuff enraged James and John to such a degree that they asked Jesus to call down fire from heaven to destroy these people. But Jesus would not listen to them; instead he rebuked them and went on to the next village.

From the time John became a disciple of Jesus, he revealed unique spiritual insight. And after he had learned much from his Lord, he became a devout and mature apostle. Nonetheless, he had to learn to focus not on his own desires and inclinations but on Jesus. Both James and John, through their mother, asked Jesus whether they might occupy the places on his right and on his left when he entered the glory of his kingdom. But Jesus refused and told them that it was not his prerogative but the Father's to assign places in his kingdom.

The fourth Gospel portrays John as a loyal follower of Jesus. Together with his brother and Peter, he belonged to the inner circle of three disciples. They were privileged to witness Jesus' raising the daughter of Jairus from the dead, Jesus' transfiguration on a mountain, and Jesus' agony in the Garden of Gethsemane.

He reciprocated love for the Lord and even describes himself as the disciple whom Jesus loved. He witnessed Jesus' crucifixion and was the first disciple to observe Jesus' empty tomb.

John's mind was both deeply religious and disarmingly simple. He knew Jesus as the Christ, the Son of God, which he made his recurring theme in his gospel. He describes the mystery of Christ's deity and humanity but leaves the solving of this ambiguity to his readers.

He observes everything in terms of contrast: good versus evil, love versus hate, heaven versus earth, light versus darkness, and life versus death. His writings, however, display a profundity similar to the depth of an ocean at the same time that they reveal the simplicity of a child. A child can read and quickly understand the words of John 3:16, but an erudite theologian has difficulty fully interpreting this text.

John as Evangelist

John is a model of modesty, for throughout the gospel, he never refers directly to either himself or his brother, James. Only in the last chapter does he mention the sons of Zebedee. Because there is no reference to John of Zebedee throughout the gospel, he does not need to identify John the Baptist but merely calls him John. The other three gospel writers carefully distinguish these two names.

In the first chapter, the author appears to indicate that he was a disciple of John the Baptist. He mentions two of John's disciples, of whom Andrew was one. They saw and heard the Baptist pointing to Jesus and saying, "Look, the Lamb of God." Then these two followed Jesus, who turned and asked, "What do you want?" They wanted to know where he was staying, and he invited them to come and see. Then these two spent the rest of the day with Jesus, from whom they learned that he was the long-expected Messiah. John switched allegiances, left John the Baptist, and became a close companion of Jesus.

Because he had mentally recorded Jesus' words and deeds, John was able to write his gospel without referring to himself yet clearly confirming that he was an eyewitness. When Jesus turned water into wine at the wedding feast in Cana, John noticed that there were six stone water jars used for ceremonial washing. He knew the capacity of each of them: twenty to thirty gallons.

When Jesus fed the multitude of five thousand, John noted the kind of bread the lad with the five loaves and two fish had: it was barley bread, an inexpensive bread eaten by poor people. When the disciples tried to row across the lake for Capernaum against a strong headwind, John knew the distance that they had rowed: three to three and a half miles.

John was in the home of Mary, Martha, and Lazarus six days before the Passover Feast. He submits an accurate eyewitness account of the incident in which Mary anointed Jesus' feet with a pint of costly perfume and wiped his feet with her hair. John reports that the entire house was filled with its fragrance. Further, he accurately records the words of Judas Iscariot, who objected to Mary's gift and called it a waste of money.

On the beach of the Lake of Galilee, John notes that the boat was only a hundred yards from shore when the disciples were towing the net full of fish. And he even gives the exact count of the large fish, 153. Again, here is the voice of a writer who indirectly makes it known that he was present at the incident.

The Disciple Whom Jesus Loved

John identifies himself five times as the disciple whom Jesus loved. First, Jesus celebrated the Passover with his disciples and then made it known that one of them would betray him. Simon Peter, who was sitting next to John, whispered to John to inquire whom Jesus meant. John asked Jesus, "Lord, who is it?" And Jesus said that he would dip a piece of bread into the dish and give it to the one who would betray him, namely, Judas Iscariot.

Next, from the cross Jesus addressed Mary and the disciple whom Jesus loved. He committed Mary to John and told him to care for her as his mother.

Third, on the first Sunday morning of Jesus' resurrection, Mary Magdalene had gone to the tomb and found that the stone had been rolled away. She immediately informed Simon Peter and the disciple whom Jesus loved. These two men ran to the tomb, but John, who was younger, reached the tomb first. He bent over, looked at the strips of cloth, but did not enter. Peter, however, entered the tomb and saw the strips of linen and the burial cloth lying separately and neatly folded. This was the cloth that had been around Jesus' head. Then John also went inside, saw what had happened, and believed that Jesus had indeed risen from the dead.

Last, twice in the account of Jesus' meeting the seven disciples on the beach of Galilee, the phrase "the disciple whom Jesus loved" appears. When these disciples, after the miraculous catch of fish, came closer to shore, John was the first to recognize Jesus standing there and said to Peter, "It's the Lord!"

After Jesus had reinstated Peter, he described how Simon would spend his days as an old man. Peter was middle-aged at his reinstatement, and some thirty-five years later, he would die a death that would glorify God. Simon looked at the disciple whom Jesus loved and asked Jesus, "Lord, what about him?" Jesus had a corrective word for Peter: "If I will that he remain until I come, what is that to you? You must follow me!"

Jesus did not want to leave the impression that the beloved disciple would not die. On the contrary, John eventually died in the city of Ephesus. He had reached an age in excess of ninety. Jesus merely wanted to say that questions about someone's future are insignificant in his sight. Obedience is what is important to him.

At the end of his gospel, John refuses to identify himself by his given name. He calls himself "this disciple," who testified that all the things that he had written were true. He reveals himself as a disciple who intensely loved the Lord and received from Jesus divine love.

Application

John was the disciple whom Jesus loved. But this does not mean that Jesus practices favoritism and that there are ranks in heaven. Of all the New Testament authors, the apostle John stresses love more than anyone else. He is the one who emphasizes Jesus' command, "Love each other as I have loved you." Love is the salient characteristic of the Christian faith.

Followers of Jesus must be known by the love they have for one another, for love is the emblem of their discipleship. But if they fail to show that distinguishing mark, their loyalty to God is nothing but pretense.

As Christians we must show the world that we are filled with love for God and our fellow human beings. The world closely watches our every move and action. When people notice Christ's love displayed in our deeds, they will have to acknowledge that we are his true witnesses. We point them to Christ, who is the source of our love.

Matthew

A Despised Tax Collector

Among intimate friends, he was known as Levi, but in the business world, his name was Matthew. He was the son of Alphaeus and a resident of Capernaum. In the list of the twelve disciples, he identifies himself as Matthew the tax collector.

In Jesus' day, a tax collector was not a position of honor among Jewish people, for it meant that he was working for the hated Roman government. Matthew had to collect the taxes not only of the local citizenry but also of the merchants who transported goods along the highway between the north and the south. His tollbooth was situated along that road.

Tax collectors were accountable to Roman government officials, but they were permitted to apply surcharges that lined their own pocketbooks. They had lucrative positions at the expense of fellow citizens, who consequently despised them. They were ostracized in Jewish society and expelled from their synagogues. They were regarded as social sinners and were placed on the same level as prostitutes, who were called moral sinners. Matthew had enriched himself and lived in a sizeable home that could accommodate many people at his banquet table. He had many tax collectors working under him, and from them he derived additional income.

Throughout his gospel, Matthew demonstrates touches of his trade. For example, his is the only Gospel account that records the incident of Peter casting his line into the lake and catching a fish with a coin in its mouth. This coin was sufficient to pay the annual temple tax for Jesus and himself. Also, in reporting the story of the Herodians' and Pharisees' asking Jesus whether it was right to pay taxes to Caesar, only Matthew relates that Jesus asked them to show him the exact coin used for paying the tax. The other evangelists say that Jesus called for a denarius, which was the common coin of the daily pay a laborer received. Moreover, Matthew was acquainted with large sums of money, as is evident in Jesus' parable of the unmerciful steward who owed his master ten thousand talents.

Early in his ministry, Jesus walked along the road where Matthew's tax booth stood. He stopped and said to its occupant, "Follow me!" Matthew stood up and right away followed Jesus. But before he left home and family, he invited Jesus and his disciples to have dinner with him and his fellow tax collectors. There were also moral and social outcasts who took a seat at the table.

Because Jesus had taken up residency in the town of Capernaum, Matthew and his companions had heard him speak and seen him perform miracles. These were the people who as outcasts of society needed a spiritual shepherd, and Jesus filled their need. The Pharisees criticized Jesus for eating a meal with these so-called sinners, but he replied, "I have come to call not the righteous but sinners to repentance." Matthew forsook his lucrative occupation, and from that moment on, he served his master with true devotion and love.

When Jesus sent forth his disciples two by two to preach the gospel, heal the sick, cleanse the lepers, raise the dead, and cast out demons, they asked him a number of questions. Matthew records that Jesus forbade them to take along a supply of gold or silver or money in their wallets. Instead, they would have to rely on God to supply all their needs.

A Meticulous Evangelist

Matthew begins his Gospel with the genealogy of Jesus to prove Christ's royal ancestry, for he is a descendant of King David. More than any other evangelist, Matthew stresses the concepts of king and kingdom throughout his gospel. He relates the question of the wise men from the East: "Where is he born king of the Jews?" In his Gospel, he records many kingdom parables. And he concludes his book with Jesus' enthronement speech: "All authority in heaven and on earth has been given to me."

But Matthew portrays Jesus not only as a king but also as a prophet. Proving that Jesus is the long-awaited Messiah promised in the Scriptures, he makes him the link between the Old and New Testaments. Sprinkling numerous quotations from the prophets throughout his Gospel, he confirms that Jesus has indeed fulfilled these messianic prophecies.

For Matthew, Jesus is the true prophet in fulfillment of God's prophecy to Moses: "I will raise up for them a prophet like you from among their brothers; I will put my words in his mouth, and he will tell them all that I command him" (Deut. 18:18). As a Jew, Matthew seeks to convince his fellow Jews that Jesus, the preacher of Nazareth, is the Christ.

Matthew notes that Jesus is the teacher who explains the Scriptures to the people at their level. Hence, the crowds heard him gladly, for he taught them as one who had authority and not as the scribes and Pharisees. Matthew succeeds in depicting Jesus as walking around with a scroll of the Old Testament in his hand and saying, "You have heard that it was said to the people long ago . . . but I tell you." Jesus came as God's spokesman with direct messages for the people. He brought them the Word of God.

As a disciple of Jesus, Matthew learned that Christ's gospel is universal; namely, it is for all people, regardless of race, color, and gender. In Jesus' genealogy, Matthew includes the names of four women who are not of Jewish descent, most of whom have less than reputable histories. They are Tamar, Rahab, Ruth, and Bathsheba, whom he lists as the unnamed wife of Uriah.

After the birth of Jesus, wise men from the East came as Gentiles to worship him with gifts of gold, incense, and myrrh. Jesus spent his early childhood not in Israel but in Egypt.

During his ministry, large crowds traveled from Gentile Decapolis to the eastern shores of the Lake of Galilee to hear him. A Roman military officer with the rank of centurion petitioned Jesus merely to speak the word to heal his ailing servant, without even entering his house. Jesus left Galilee and, traveling north to the region of Tyre and Sidon, healed the daughter of a Gentile woman. When Jesus was exhausted on his way to Golgotha, a black man from Cyrene in North Africa carried the cross.

Only Matthew's gospel records the Great Commission, in which Jesus says to make disciples of all nations.

Application

The portrait that Matthew draws of Jesus is that he is Lord of all peoples. He is the majestic King, the true Prophet, the gentle Shepherd, the great Physician, and the patient Teacher. He indeed is the Messiah, the fulfiller of all of God's promises.

Jesus breaks down racial, cultural, and linguistic barriers and unites his people around the globe. This means that his people too must follow Jesus in accepting fellow Christians, regardless of background, color, and status. Jesus stresses the unity of the body of Christ, of which we are living members.

PAUL THE PHARISEE

ACTS 7–9, 22, AND 26

An Enviable Education

Paul was born into a Jewish family living in dispersion in the city of Tarsus, which was located in the province of Cilicia, the southeastern province of Asia Minor (modern Turkey). His father or grandfather had gained Roman citizenship as a reward for aiding the Roman forces that had come to occupy that part of Asia Minor. The reward stipulated that citizenship be passed on to future generations. Thus, Paul was born a Roman citizen, which for him was of great benefit in later life.

His parents were able to trace their heritage back to the tribe of Benjamin, in which King Saul featured as a prominent figure. They therefore named their son Saul, a name that in Hebrew was pronounced Saoul. At birth, Saul was also given the Greek name Paul, which was used in Gentile contexts. On his first missionary journey on the island of Cyprus, Saul saw the necessity of having people call him by his Greek name, Paul, to be an effective missionary among the Gentiles.

As a teenager leaving his home to study religion in Jerusalem, Paul was fluent in four languages: Aramaic, Hebrew, Greek, and Latin. He

157

learned Greek as a child in his native Tarsus. In his parental home, Aramaic was spoken, while in the synagogue, he learned Hebrew. From the Romans in his city, he gained a working knowledge of Latin. Because Tarsus had a thriving university in which Stoic philosophy was taught, the possibility is real that Paul became thoroughly acquainted with Greek culture and customs.

Paul studied theology in Jerusalem under the renowned scholar Gamaliel II, who was a member of the lenient faction of Pharisees. Paul, however, became a member of the faction that was strict in doctrine and practice, because his father also belonged to that party.

Paul learned the Scriptures by heart and cultivated the ability to interpret them, so that throughout his life he could recite them from memory and explain them. It is not unrealistic to think that as a student in Jerusalem, Paul had occasionally heard Jesus teach near the temple in Solomon's Colonnade. But being influenced by his strict party affiliation, he resolutely rejected Christ's gospel. When the followers of Jesus began to multiply in Jerusalem and Judea, he arrested them and brought them before the Jewish authorities to be tried, punished, and, in some cases, executed. And Paul cast his vote in favor of putting them to death.

Roadside Transformation

When Paul was about thirty years of age, he began to assume responsibilities. He took part in the stoning of an ardent follower of Jesus named Stephen. When Stephen's accusers were by law required to throw the first stones at the man, he became the guardian of their cloaks. Soon after the death of Christianity's first martyr, Paul was increasingly involved in persecuting Christians. Then came the day when the high priest sent him to Damascus on a mission to arrest adherents of the Way, as Christians were called. Paul had to bring these people to Jerusalem to stand trial, be lashed, or be killed.

When they came within sight of Damascus, a brilliant light from heaven suddenly flashed around him and caused him to fall to the ground. Then he heard a voice calling him in Hebrew, "Saul, Saul, why do you persecute me?"

He sensed that a heavenly voice was speaking to him, so he asked for clarification: "Who are you, Lord?" He realized that the voice speaking to him was Jesus, the ascended Lord, for he knew that he had risen from the dead and had ascended to heaven. Paul struggled with a number of questions:

- Why did Jesus identify himself with the persecuted Christians?
- Why did Jesus use the personal pronoun "me"?
- Were God and Jesus one in essence?

Paul was confused, for he thought that he was doing God a favor by persecuting the Christians. Why did Jesus express disapproval of his ambition to offer a service to God? He knew the Old Testament Scriptures by heart, avidly defended the purity of God's Word, and faithfully recited the creed: "Hear, O Israel: The Lord our God, the Lord is one" (Deut. 6:4). This creed precluded a doctrine of God who had a Son equal to him. To Paul, proclaiming Jesus as the Son of God was utter blasphemy that had to be punished with execution.

Jesus answered Paul and said to him, "Yes, indeed, I am Jesus, whom you are persecuting!" All at once Paul recalled the words spoken by Stephen just before he was stoned to death: "Look, I see heaven opened and the Son of Man standing at the right hand of God." And in his dying moments, Stephen had said, "Lord Jesus, receive my spirit." Now Paul realized that the living Jesus confronted him and was speaking on behalf of his followers. Paul was sinning against Jesus by persecuting the Christians. Twice Jesus accused Paul of persecuting him, for Jesus and the Christians are one.

Jesus did not stop there but told Paul what to do. He said, "Now get up and enter the city, and you will be told what to do." Jesus did not yet give him further instructions, namely to join the fellowship of Christians in Damascus, become an apostle to the Gentiles, and suffer for Jesus.

Paul's companions heard the voice but were unable to understand what was said. They had to help Paul get up and then realized that he was blind. They had to take him by the hand, lead him into the city, and leave him in the house of Judas, who lived in a house on

Straight Street. There he sat for three days without eating or drinking. Unable to see, he needed time to reflect. Note the following changes in his life:

- Paul, who had wanted to run the Christians into the ground, now had lain face down on the ground.
- Paul, who had wanted to bind Christians and lead them as prisoners from Damascus to Jerusalem, now was imprisoned in darkness in Damascus.
- Paul, who had acted with authority from the high priest in Jerusalem, now had to break ties with the high priest.
- And last, Paul, who had wanted to persecute the Christians in Damascus, now had to receive physical and spiritual help from these Christians.

In brilliant glory light, Jesus confronted Paul, who was spiritually blind. In contrast Paul, who was physically blind for three days, came to Jesus and saw him spiritually. Everything in Paul's life was turned upside down.

Then Jesus appeared to a devout Christian in Damascus named Ananias and instructed him to go to the house of Judas. There he had to ask for a man by the name of Paul, who had prayed to Jesus and in a vision had seen a man named Ananias come to lay his hands on him so that he might regain his sight.

The reports concerning Paul's coming to Damascus to arrest the Christians had circulated throughout the region, and all the believers there were prepared for attacks against them. And then in the midst of all these anxieties and fears, Jesus instructed Ananias to go to meet Paul and heal him of his blindness.

Ananias registered his objections to Jesus, for the harm Paul had wreaked on the Christians in Jerusalem and Judea was well known. Jesus took no offense but told Ananias to go to Paul for the following two reasons: Paul was Jesus' chosen instrument to bring the gospel to the Gentiles, kings, and the people of Israel; and Paul would have to suffer for the name of Jesus.

Jesus chose Paul to be the apostle to the Gentiles because he was the right person to present him best. Paul was fluent in Aramaic, Hebrew, Greek, and Latin. As a Jew, he was well trained in the Scriptures and had the equivalent of a doctorate in Old Testament studies. He was thoroughly familiar with the customs of the Greek-speaking world and could present the gospel in their culture. In addition, he was a Roman citizen who could freely travel along the Roman highways to spread the Good News throughout the empire. He was the right man in the right post at the right time.

Application

Of all Jesus' apostles, none had the background, education, training, and position that Paul had. None but Paul would have been able to serve God as a missionary to the Gentiles. He planted churches in various places, counseled Jews and Gentiles, wrote letters that are part of the New Testament, and trained pastors. Paul was a man prepared by God.

None of us are able to write the script for our lives. Yet when we look back, we see the hand of God leading, guiding, and preparing us. We must confess that God in his providence has prepared us for productive service in his church and kingdom. And we thank him for his abundant blessings.

Paul the Apostle

Acts 9, 22, and 26

Paul's Early Life as a Christian

Ever since his ascension, Jesus has directed from heaven the development of his church here on earth. He sends his angels to communicate messages to his people, or he appears personally in a dream or vision. The Lord is fully in control of his worldwide church.

Jesus sent Ananias to restore Paul's sight so that Paul would be filled with the Holy Spirit. Also, he came to Paul in a vision and confirmed that he was sending him to both Jews and Gentiles and that he would rescue Paul from violent attacks.

He instructed Paul to preach the gospel to Jews and Gentiles, open their spiritual eyes, and turn them from darkness to light, from the power of Satan to God. Then Jesus would graciously extend to Jews and Gentiles the gift of forgiveness of sins. He would grant them an inheritance among all those whom he had sanctified through his atoning blood.

Immediately after his conversion, Paul was filled with the Holy Spirit and went to local churches. Ananias paved the way for this new disciple, who had to prove that his conversion was genuine. Paul preached from the Old Testament Scriptures that Jesus of Nazareth fulfilled the messianic prophecies and thus is the Son of God.

Paul had to flee Damascus and went into the Arabian Desert. He stayed for three years, then returned to Damascus, where threats on his life became even more pronounced than before he had left. The time had come for him to escape at night in a basket over the city wall and return to Jerusalem.

When Paul arrived in Jerusalem, he had to face the Christians whom he had persecuted a few years earlier and who were deathly afraid of him. Also, even if he should think of meeting the high priest, he would be accused of being a traitor to the Jewish cause. He had no place to go in the city of Jerusalem.

Barnabas befriended Paul and brought him into the fellowship of the Christians and into the company of the apostles. He was an encourager who saw the hand of the Lord in Paul's life and on that basis introduced Paul to Peter and James, telling them that he fearlessly preached in the Damascus synagogues that Jesus is the Son of God.

Paul stayed with Peter and James for fifteen days, learning from Peter the gospel of Jesus and Jesus' parables and discourses. Paul knew the Old Testament Scriptures by heart and understood that Jesus had fulfilled the messianic prophecies. But he had not had the privilege of being instructed by Jesus. Therefore he was now a disciple of one of his apostles so that in time he could go forth as an apostle to the Gentiles, preaching and teaching Jesus' gospel.

The Mantle of Apostleship

While in Jerusalem, Paul went to the same Greek-speaking synagogues where Stephen had preached and had been arrested. Paul spoke boldly in the name of Jesus but immediately received death threats, to the point that he had to flee the city. When Paul was praying in the temple, Jesus came to him in a vision and said, "Hurry and quickly leave Jerusalem, because they will not accept your testimony about me. Go, I will send you far away to the Gentiles." Fellow

Christians took him to the port city of Caesarea and put him aboard a ship to his hometown, Tarsus.

When Paul arrived there, he did not sit still but preached the Word of God throughout the province of Cilicia and also in the northern part of Syria. Unfortunately, there is little known about Paul's missionary activities prior to his call by Barnabas to come to the growing and developing church in Antioch of Syria and help him with the work of teaching the Scriptures.

After Paul had taught for a whole year with Barnabas, the Holy Spirit called both of them to be missionaries to the Gentiles. Together with Mark, the writer of the Gospel, they went to the island of Cyprus, the birthplace of Barnabas. With Paul as leader and spokesman, they brought the Good News to the Roman proconsul Sergius Paulus. This Roman official was the first Gentile believer who came to faith in Jesus Christ. It is interesting to note that in this context, Paul dropped the name Saul. He was now officially Jesus' apostle to the Gentiles.

From Cyprus, Paul and his companions sailed north to Asia Minor (modern Turkey) and went to Antioch in Pisidia, where Paul preached the gospel in the synagogue. When they returned to this synagogue a week later, the Jewish leaders derided Paul and Barnabas by contradicting the message of the gospel that Jesus is the Son of God. At that point, Paul declared that they would go to the Gentiles. And among these people, Paul and Barnabas started churches in Iconium, Lystra, and Derbe.

Jesus never forsook Paul, for he stood next to him in all the trials he had to endure. During his second missionary journey, Paul brought the gospel to Corinth, which was a city known for its blatant immorality. Jewish authorities rebuffed him and drove him out of the synagogue. Paul was greatly discouraged, but during the night, Jesus spoke to him and said, "Do not be afraid, but continue to speak and do not be silent. For I am with you, and no one is going to attack you to harm you, because I have many people in this city." Paul stayed in Corinth for eighteen months and established a thriving church there.

When Paul completed his third missionary journey, he returned to Jerusalem and within days was arrested and brought before the

Sanhedrin because of his ministry to the Gentiles. As Paul spoke in defense of himself, his opponents physically assaulted him. If the Roman commander and his soldiers had not rescued him, he would have been torn to pieces. Then during the night, Jesus appeared to Paul and said, "Take courage! As you have witnessed about me in Jerusalem, so you must witness in Rome" (Acts 23:11).

On his voyage to Rome, Paul and 275 other shipmates were in a violent storm for two weeks in the middle of the Mediterranean Sea. When all hope was lost and everyone feared a watery grave, Paul stood up and addressed his shipmates. He said that during the night, an angel of the Lord Jesus Christ had instructed him not to be afraid, for he would have to stand trial before the Roman emperor, and that not one of them would lose their lives in the storm.

The words of this angel reinforced Jesus' earlier message that Paul would stand trial in Rome. Although the New Testament provides no information on this trial, we do know that Paul was set free and traveled to Spain, Crete, Greece, and Asia Minor. He was a tireless preacher of the gospel who pleaded with Jews and Gentiles to accept Jesus Christ.

Paul was instrumental in bringing the gospel to the ends of the then-known world. While he spent two years in house arrest in Rome, he was chained to a Roman soldier. Paul wasted no time acquainting the soldier with Jesus Christ and taught him the gospel. As is common in the military, soldiers are transferred. Likewise this soldier who now had become a follower of Jesus Christ was sent to France and had an opportunity to tell others about Jesus. In the course of time, Paul brought numerous soldiers to Christ. As they went forth to various parts of the Roman Empire, the gospel spread throughout the empire.

Application

In the service of his Lord, Paul planted churches in Philippi, Thessalonica, Berea, Corinth, and Ephesus. He traveled to countries that are known today as Lebanon, Syria, Turkey, Greece, Albania, Yugoslavia, Italy, Spain, and the islands of Crete, Cyprus, and Malta.

At the end of his life, he wrote, "I have fought the good fight, I have finished the race, I have kept the faith" (2 Tim. 4:7). He was indeed the champion of the Christian faith.

Jesus has instructed us to stand firm to the end, with the result that we will be saved. By implication, he tells us that he is standing next to us in our trials, hardships, adversities, and triumphs. He is the author and perfecter of our faith. He has given us the promise that he will never leave us and never forsake us.

People Whose Lives Jesus Touched

MARY

An Archangel's Visit

As was customary in her culture, Mary married young. She was only fifteen when she was engaged to a young man named Joseph in the Galilean town of Nazareth, where both had grown up. Joseph was a carpenter by trade. Both of them loved God and sought to live in obedience to his commandments. They knew the Scriptures and faithfully attended the worship services in their synagogue.

The religious custom in those days was that a prospective husband and wife would exchange vows of fidelity in a premarital ceremony. This meant that they would have to live in abstinence before the wedding day and the consummation of their marriage If this relationship were broken during that period, it would be regarded as a divorce with legal implications.

Then one day, God sent his angel Gabriel to Mary with a greeting and the message that she was highly favored, for the Lord was with her. This notice caused her to be perplexed, because she had no idea why she as a teenage girl was highly favored in God's sight.

169

Mary was troubled and did not know how to respond to Gabriel's message. She patiently waited for additional information. Gabriel spoke reassuring words: "Don't be afraid, Mary, for God is gracious to you." But then he proceeded to give her a message that overwhelmed her. He said, "You will conceive in your womb and give birth to a son, and you will call him Jesus. He will be great and will be called the Son of the Most High. And the Lord God will give him the throne of his father David. He will rule over the house of Jacob forever, and his kingdom will never end."

Mary tried to imagine what it meant that as descendants of King David, she and Joseph would have a son who would be king in an everlasting kingdom. She had no difficulty with the name Jesus, for it was the equivalent of the Hebrew name Joshua. She marveled at the news that God would choose this name for her future son. But what did Gabriel mean when he said that her son would be great and be called Son of the Most High?

Mary continued to reflect on Gabriel's prediction, but suddenly it dawned on her that she was running ahead of herself—she was not even married. She said to Gabriel, "How can this be, because I am a virgin?" She expressed no unbelief, only bewilderment. How could she lawfully conceive a baby apart from a husband? Gabriel continued his missive from God and said, "The Holy Spirit will come upon you, and the power of the Most High will overshadow you. Therefore the holy child to be born will be called the Son of God."

Here is a mystery that no human being is able to understand fully and interpret adequately. Mary accepted the message in faith that God through the Holy Spirit would be the Father of the child to be born. Hence the child would be a divine offspring dwelling in a body formed in the womb of Mary. As a divine child called Son of the Most High, he would be born and live without sin and thus rule in his everlasting kingdom.

Mary would have to inform Joseph about the angelic visit and tell him that she would conceive, bear a son, and give him the name Jesus. Joseph heard her story and was shocked to know that his fiancée was pregnant with a child that was not his. It was too much for him. Even though he dearly loved Mary, he saw no other way out than to quietly end their engagement, namely, to avoid any legal proceedings and not hurt her in any way.

As he tossed and turned at night, unable to sleep, an angel of the Lord came to him in a dream. The angel said, "Joseph, son of David, do not hesitate to take Mary as your wife, for what is conceived in her is from the Holy Spirit. She will give birth to a son, and you are to call him Jesus, for he will save his people from their sins."

Joseph was dumbfounded because he received more or less the same information Mary had heard from the angel Gabriel. These were references to King David, conception through the Holy Spirit, the birth of a son, and the name Jesus. Also, the angel told him not to worry, just as Gabriel had instructed Mary not to be afraid. The matter was from God and not the result of sinful human acts.

Elizabeth's Exultation

At the beginning of her pregnancy, Mary decided to travel from Nazareth to the hill country of Judea to the south of Jerusalem and stay with relatives for some time. This decision, made with Joseph's approval, shielded her from embarrassment in Nazareth, where gossip and malicious words could severely hurt her.

Mary wanted to visit her blood relative Elizabeth, who was married to the priest Zechariah and was well past childbearing age. The angel Gabriel had informed Mary that Elizabeth had conceived a child and was already in her sixth month of pregnancy. These two women wanted to talk about their individual pregnancies: the one as a teenager and the other as an elderly woman.

Elizabeth, filled with the Holy Spirit, cried out and said that Mary was blessed among women because of the special child in her womb. She called Mary "the mother of my Lord," for the child in Elizabeth's womb jumped for joy upon hearing Mary's greeting. Elizabeth continued and said that Mary was blessed because she believed the words that God through his angel had spoken to her.

Mary stayed with Elizabeth and Zechariah for about three months and then left for Nazareth.

The Birth of Jesus

Emperor Caesar Augustus had issued a decree that all citizens in the Roman Empire had to be registered in the town where they were born. Joseph and Mary, now married, both had their roots in Bethlehem in Judea and had to travel there to be registered.

When they finally arrived in Bethlehem, there was no place for them in the inn. There was not even room for them in houses owned by relatives. One area that was not occupied was a stable that had some straw and an empty feeding trough.

Mary made it known to Joseph that the time had come for Jesus to be born. The place where they could spend the night provided privacy, yet the lack of all conveniences for Mary to give birth to her son portrayed utter poverty. She wrapped her firstborn in strips of cloth and laid him on a bed of straw in a manger.

They knew the Scripture that predicted the birth of Jesus: "But you, Bethlehem Ephrathah, you who are small among the clans of Judah, from you will come for me one who will be ruler over Israel, whose origins are from of old, from ancient days" (Micah 5:2). They worried not about poverty but rejoiced that God had fulfilled his promise and had given them the privilege of caring for Jesus.

That same night, shepherds who had been out in the field watching over their flock came to the stable. Excitedly, these humble men reported that a bit earlier an angel of the Lord had come to them in brilliant heavenly light with the message not to be frightened. The angel had spoken of great joy for all people, because in the town of David, namely, Bethlehem, Christ the Lord was born. He even had given them directions for where to find the baby wrapped in cloth and lying in a manger.

While the angel was speaking, suddenly a multitude of angels came down out of heaven. Together they were praising God and saying, "Glory to God in the highest, and on earth peace among people, with whom he is pleased."

The shepherds had immediately identified the precise place and hurried to where Mary, Joseph, and the baby were. They were the first to pay homage to the Christ, the Son of God.

Mary and Jesus

After Jesus was born, Mary and Joseph and the child stayed with relatives in a home for forty days. At that time, the days of purification were completed, according to the Mosaic law, and then Joseph and Mary traveled to the temple in Jerusalem. They presented Jesus to God with a prescribed sacrifice of either two turtledoves or two young pigeons.

At the temple, an elderly gentleman named Simeon met them. He was known to be righteous and devout and one who waited for the salvation of Israel. He was filled with the Holy Spirit, who had told him that he would not die before he saw God's anointed Son. The Spirit guided him to the temple, where he met Joseph and Mary and Jesus. Simeon took the infant in his arms, and blessing God, he said, "Now, Lord, you are releasing your servant in peace, according to your word. Because my eyes have seen your salvation that you have prepared in the presence of all the peoples, a light for revelation to the Gentiles, and a glory for your people, Israel." Simeon spoke of Jesus' birth as being significant not only for Israel but for the whole world. He blessed Joseph and Mary and then addressed Mary in a prophecy about her son: "This child is destined for the fall and rising of many in Israel and for a sign that will be opposed—a sword will pierce your own soul, too—that the deliberations of many hearts may be revealed."

An elderly widow known as Anna also approached Joseph and Mary and the baby. She thanked God for Jesus' birth and then spoke about the child to everyone who was waiting for the salvation of Jerusalem. Both Simeon and Anna knew that they had seen the Messiah and God's promises fulfilled in him.

When Joseph, Mary, and the child returned to Bethlehem, wise men from the East came to pay homage to Jesus, whom they honored as king. The men had seen a star, and as astronomers, they interpreted this to mean that a king had been born in the land of the Jews. They had traveled to Jerusalem and inquired at the palace of King Herod the Great where this royal child might be. Herod called together the learned leaders of the Jews and inquired where this child would be born.

Herod instructed the wise men to travel another six miles in a southerly direction and go to Bethlehem. They went in the evening and saw that the star was going ahead of them. It stopped when they arrived at the house where Jesus was.

The men entered the house and saw the child with his mother, Mary. They bowed down to the ground and worshiped him. Led by the Spirit of God, they acknowledged him as king, as a special king of the Jews. They paid the baby their deepest respects by honoring him with gifts fit for royalty: gold, frankincense, and myrrh.

These wise men returned to their homeland via a different route, and Joseph with Mary and the child left for Egypt, where they stayed until they heard that Herod had died. After his death, Joseph with Mary and Jesus returned to the land of Israel, but because Herod's son Archelaus was ruler in Judea, they went to Galilee, where they settled safely in Nazareth.

Jesus grew up in the town of Nazareth. When he was twelve years old, his father and mother took him to Jerusalem to take part in the Feast of Passover. At the age of twelve, Jesus was a precocious child who debated the learned spiritual leaders of Israel.

When the Passover Feast came to an end, Joseph and Mary started on their way back to Nazareth and assumed that Jesus was traveling with friends his age. But after they had been on the road for a day, they could not find him, not knowing that Jesus had stayed behind in Jerusalem. Going back to the city, they found him in the temple, seated among the learned teachers of the law.

Mary could not restrain herself and reprimanded Jesus for neglecting to tell his parents where he was. "Child, why did you do this to us? Look, your father and I worried ourselves sick looking for you." She expressed her motherly concern and their parental responsibility for Jesus. But he looked at the matter from his point of view and in his answer indicated that she should have known where he was and what he was doing. He asked, "Why were you looking for me? Didn't you know that I had to be in my Father's house?"

By referring to his heavenly Father, Jesus made known his divine descent. Mary did not forget this incident and the words Jesus spoke. She stored all these details in her memory, and with her reflective mind, she would recall them and meditate on them, especially at the time Jesus was nailed to the cross. At that moment, a sword went through her heart when she realized that he was going back to his

Father. And from the cross, Jesus committed Mary to the loving care of John, the son of Zebedee. He loved his mother and provided for her needs even as his earthly life was coming to an end.

Application

Luke accurately describes Mary's spiritual condition: she treasured in her heart all the words concerning Jesus and reflected on them. She lived in the presence of the Son of God and contemplated the mystery of the divine and human in the person of her offspring. The living words came to her through angels and from the lips of Jesus. Mary guarded these words as spiritual treasures in her heart. Her spirit rejoiced in God her Savior.

Being his mother, Mary was close to her son, but as a sinner, she like everyone else needed him as her Savior. There is then no favoritism with Jesus, for he is just as close to Mary as he is to all his followers.

Jesus is as close to us today as he was to his mother in her day. He gave us this promise when he ascended to heaven: "Remember, I am with you all the days until the end of time." He will never break his promise, for he stands next to everyone who comes to him in prayer.

MARY MAGDALENE

A Grateful Follower of Jesus

Mary Magdalene derived her name from the town of her birth, Magdala (also known as Magadan), which is situated along the western shore of the Lake of Galilee. Jesus had visited this area after he had miraculously fed the four thousand.

She was among the women healed by Jesus of evil spirits and various diseases. Because of these demons, her life had been far from normal. When Jesus freed her from these evil spirits, she expressed her undying gratitude to him.

With other women, Mary Magdalene showed her thankfulness to Jesus. From her own resources, she supported and helped him in his ministry. She stood out among the others by being present when Jesus suffered on the cross. She watched where Nicodemus and Joseph of Arimathea laid Jesus to rest in the tomb, and very early on Sunday morning, she went to the tomb to anoint Jesus' body. Late Friday afternoon, just before the Sabbath began at six o'clock, the task of preparing Jesus' body for proper burial was not completed. Thus this responsibility would have to wait until early Sunday morning, the first day of the week.

176

On Easter Sunday, when Jesus rose from the grave, Mary Magdalene went to the tomb before daybreak. She was not alone, for other women accompanied her. When they arrived, she noticed that the stone had been removed. Mary wondered how that had happened, because Governor Pontius Pilate had ordered the tombstone secured with a seal and guarded by soldiers.

Mary failed to look into the tomb as the other women did. Alarmed, she rushed back into the city to tell Peter and John that the stone had been rolled away from the grave. Terrified, she said, "They have taken the Lord out of the tomb, and we don't know where they have put him."

Peter and John immediately rushed to the garden tomb, but as the younger of the two, John was able to run faster than Peter and arrived there first. He looked through the low entrance and noticed the linen bandages lying there, but he did not enter. Peter, however, came right behind him, went inside, and saw not only the linen bandages but also the burial cloth that had covered Jesus' head. He noticed that the burial cloth was put in a separate place. The bandages, cloth, and spices were sufficient proof that thieves had not taken the body away, for they would have removed everything.

The Compassionate Risen Lord

When Peter and John returned to Jerusalem, a weeping Mary Magdalene returned to the tomb. Quietly sobbing, she walked over to the entrance, stooped to look inside, and then saw two angels in white garments sitting at the head and feet of where Jesus' body had lain. The color of white should have alerted her that these two were not men but angels. But because of her confused mind, she failed to notice their apparel.

The angels asked her why she was weeping. She responded, "They have taken away my Lord, and I do not know where they have put him." Mary repeated the same words she had spoken to Peter and John in Jerusalem. Now she referred to Jesus as her Lord. But she did not realize that her Lord was standing right next to her, since she did not recognize him through her tear-filled eyes.

Jesus addressed her and asked her why she was crying and for whom she was looking. Still there was no recognition, for she thought that the gardener was standing next to her. She said, "Sir, if you have carried him away, tell me where you have laid him, and I will get him." She heard a male voice and dimly saw a male figure, but still she was confused.

Then Jesus spoke and said, "Mary." That one word was all she needed to be brought back to reality. She immediately recognized Jesus' voice. She lifted her head and saw him standing right in front of her. All she could do was to stammer one word in her Aramaic dialect: "*Rabbouni,*" which means Teacher.

Mary put her arms around Jesus and clung to him in an effort not to let him depart from her. But Jesus wanted her to understand that a fundamental change had taken place not in their personal relationship but in actuality. His earthly citizenship had come to an end with his death, so to speak. His heavenly citizenship became reality with his resurrection. Mary had to understand that even though she embraced him now, she could not keep him on this earth, because he would ascend to his Father.

Jesus gave these instructions to Mary: "Go to my brothers and tell them, 'I am ascending to my Father and your Father, to my God and your God.'" Jesus wanted her to convey a message that had far-reaching implications: the time had come for him to ascend and permanently depart to his Father. He now regarded the disciples as his brothers and told them that his Father was their Father and his God was their God. He did not mean to say that there were no differences. Jesus is the one and only Son of the Father, but his disciples are adopted sons and daughters. He is the true Son of God, while believers are children of God.

Application

After his ascension, Jesus would be spiritually near to all his brothers and sisters. The fellowship Mary had enjoyed would remain, but it would become much more meaningful in the future.

"I have seen the Lord!" These are the words Mary Magdalene spoke when she came to the disciples that first Easter Sunday. Countless people around the globe utter a slightly different message. They say, "I have met the Lord and he has saved me!" Seeing and meeting Jesus is one of the most pronounced blessings in the life of a Christian. Nothing compares with knowing Jesus Christ as Lord and Savior.

Two People of Emmaus

LUKE 24

The Stranger

Two people were walking from Jerusalem on their homeward way. One was named Cleopas, and the other unidentified person may have been his wife. As devout Jews, they had gone to the capital to celebrate the annual Feast of Passover in the capital city.

When the festivities were over, they traveled back to the village of Emmaus, which was located about seven miles to the northwest of Jerusalem. This distance could be traversed within three hours, which would mean that they left the city midafternoon and were home before nightfall.

As they were walking, they discussed the crucifixion of Jesus and the report of his resurrection. They were unable to grasp the meaning of all that they had seen and heard. They were filled with sorrow about the death of Jesus but were confused about the various accounts they had heard that he was seen alive. As they were intensely engaged in conversation, they had not paid any attention to someone walking alongside of them. They merely acknowledged him as a stranger whom they did not recognize.

When the stranger wished to enter their discussion, he asked them what the topic of their conversation was. This question took them by such surprise that they stopped in their tracks. He must have overheard some of their talk and thus could have guessed what topic captivated their attention. He must have heard their sad voices and seen their gloomy faces.

Where had this stranger been the last three days when everybody in and around Jerusalem talked about Jesus' crucifixion, and the period of darkness and the earthquake that occurred the day before the Sabbath began? Moreover, throughout the day the latest news had been about the empty grave and the report of Jesus' appearing to women and to his disciples.

Cleopas asked him outright, "Are you the only visitor to Jerusalem who did not become acquainted with the things that have happened in it these days?"

But the stranger asked, "What things?"

Then they told him what had happened to Jesus, the prophet from Nazareth in Galilee.

This prophet had been a true God-ordained teacher of the Scriptures and the greatest miracle-worker in the presence of all the people. He had addressed multitudes of people and even raised the dead back to life. Among those who were raised to life was Lazarus of Bethany. But the ruling clergy and Jewish officials of the Sanhedrin in Jerusalem had handed Jesus over to Pontius Pilate, the Roman governor. And at their request, he had sentenced Jesus to death by nailing him to a wooden cross.

Cleopas and his companion shared with the stranger their disappointment in Jesus. They had hoped that this prophet of God, mighty in word and deed, would have been the one to set them free from Roman occupation. "In addition," they said, "it is now the third day since these things have taken place." Their hopes had been dashed when Jesus died on that cross three days earlier.

Then they shared the latest news. They said that in spite of the gloom and doom of the past week, early that same morning some of their women had gone to the tomb and found it empty. These women had come to complete the preparation of the body for proper burial, but they did not find the body of Jesus. Instead, they had seen angels who told them that Jesus was alive.

Also, some of their friends had gone to the tomb to verify what the women had reported. These men had found that the women had given an accurate report, for the body of Jesus was not there.

Breaking Bread

The stranger listened as they were walking toward Emmaus. When he began to speak, his words were reproachful. He said, "O how foolish and slow of heart you are to believe everything that the prophets have spoken! Was it not necessary for the Christ to suffer these things and then to enter into his glory?" He berated them for failing to understand the Scriptures, which gave them all the information they needed about the suffering and resurrection of the Messiah. Instead of exercising their intellectual acumen and understanding the written Word of God, they stumbled in spiritual darkness and wrapped themselves in a cloak of ignorance.

Then the stranger, who seemed to have memorized the sacred Scriptures, showed the two people of Emmaus what God's Word said about the suffering and glory of the Messiah. He began with the books of Moses and went on to the prophetic books to disclose how the Messiah had fulfilled everything that had been written about him.

When they approached the village of Emmaus, the sun had set and the day had come to an end. The husband and his wife were going to their home, but the stranger acted as if he were going farther. In typical Mideastern fashion, they urged their companion to enter their abode and spend the night there. They pressed him to accept their invitation and thus be assured of safety, food and drink, and a warm bed. Anything less would have been a breach of hospitality.

At the home of the host and hostess, the wife prepared the evening meal. When the time came to be seated at the table, they asked their guest to bless the food. And this is what he did: he took the bread, broke it, and then gave the broken pieces to each of them.

They observed the manner in which he broke the bread and gave it to them, and then they saw the marks in his hands.

Suddenly they recognized Jesus. This stranger was no one else but the risen Lord. How could they have been so dense while they walked with him for more than two hours and conversed about the Messiah revealed in the Scriptures! But as they recognized him, he suddenly vanished from their sight.

Now that their spiritual eyes were opened, they talked excitedly about all that had transpired. They asked each other, "Were not our hearts burning within us as he was talking to us on the way while he opened the Scriptures to us?" As they reflected on Jesus' teaching, they readily admitted that their hearts had been stirred and set on fire as their understanding of the Word had increased.

They could now declare that the report of the women concerning the empty tomb was accurate. And they considered their time with the risen Lord a great privilege. Without knowing it, they had entertained the glorified Jesus in their own home.

Now that they understood that Jesus had risen indeed, they could not keep this knowledge to themselves. Without giving another thought to the hazards of traveling at night, they left their home and ran back to Jerusalem as fast as they could. They covered the distance in half the time it took them to travel home.

In Jerusalem, they went straight to the place where the disciples were gathered. When they were admitted, for the door of the room was locked for fear of the Jews, they were ready to blurt out that they had seen Jesus and that he was risen indeed. But they were unable to do so because they found the disciples in an exhilarated state. These people exclaimed that the Lord had risen indeed and that he had appeared to Simon. And they did not even have to add that the report of the women was true and that the grave was empty.

The two of Emmaus were finally given the opportunity to relate their story. They told the disciples what had happened to them on the way home and how they had walked and talked with a stranger who opened the Scriptures and taught them about the Messiah. Then they described what had happened at the evening meal: how Jesus had taken the bread, blessed it, and had given it to them. Their eyes were opened, and they recognized Jesus, their resurrected Lord.

Their excitement had been so strong that they could not keep it to themselves but had to return to Jerusalem and share the good news with Jesus' disciples.

Application

The twosome from Emmaus would never forget this glorious incident of being taught by Jesus, sharing a meal with him, and recognizing him as their risen Savior. They would go forth until the day of their deaths and be witnesses of Jesus' resurrection. They indeed were his eyewitnesses, who had seen, heard, and touched him.

The word *witness* had a dual meaning for them. It means to see and to testify. Today, believers see Jesus spiritually, and they bear witness that he has risen indeed.

We seize any and every opportunity Jesus gives us and are witnesses for him. He calls us to testify for him in whatever capacity this may be, whether at home or work, in school, on the road, and even in times of relaxation. Jesus wants us to be his living witnesses in word and deed.

Rich Young Man

MATTHEW 19 AND LUKE 18

Born Rich but Unhappy

He was born into a rich family, received a good education, knew the Scriptures, and was a law-abiding citizen, a prominent citizen, and a relatively young man. He belonged to the ruling class of Jewish society. His social decorum and virtuous conduct added to a successful life. Blessed with keen intellect and a proactive disposition, he excelled in whatever he initiated. Consequently, his material possessions multiplied so that he was counted among the rich people in Israel. In many respects, success had brought him to the top of the economic world.

Nonetheless, he knew that his success had failed to make him happy He was aware of an emptiness that had left a hollow feeling in his inner being. He realized that when he died, his possessions would be unable to help him in the afterlife.

What would he have to do to prepare himself for the hereafter? Although he was a religious person and attended the worship services at the synagogue, this persistent dissatisfaction in his spiritual life kept

185

bothering him to such a degree that he needed spiritual counsel. When he heard that Jesus was coming through the area, he immediately realized that this Galilean teacher would be able to help him. Having been in the audience when Jesus preached, he was greatly impressed with his straightforward manner of teaching the Scriptures.

If only he could get near to Jesus, he would ask him a question that had been on his mind for a long time. Suddenly he saw his opportunity when Jesus was not occupied. He ran up to him and out of deep respect fell on his knees in front of him.

The young ruler asked, "Good teacher, what must I do to inherit eternal life?" He was striving to live a morally upright life, and he was privileged to have inherited riches. These two thoughts demanded top priority in his mind, and thus he included them in his question. He had inherited earthly possessions because his father upon his death had bequeathed the estate to his son. Now the young man asked Jesus how he could inherit life in the hereafter.

His commendable question reveals vital concerns on how to live now and how to get oneself ready for life after death. This earthly life is comparatively short, whereas eternal life has no end and is heavenly. The term *life eternal* is equivalent to salvation. It means to be forever in the presence of God, enjoying the riches of heaven.

Jesus had a straightforward and succinct answer for the young man. He asked, "Why do you call me good? No one is good except one, namely, God." Jesus pointed to the origin of goodness. He directed the young ruler's attention to God and his law. The source of all that is good is God, from whom all earthly and heavenly blessings flow.

Often in his teaching, Jesus referred to the Ten Commandments, which every human being must uphold and obey. What then did the young man have to do to become an heir to salvation? Jesus had the answer ready for him: "You know the commandments: Do not kill. Do not commit adultery. Do not steal. Do not bear false testimony. Do not defraud. Honor your father and your mother."

The young man knew and honored these basic rules; they were regularly taught in synagogues and religious settings. He could testify that he had led a moral and upright life and had obeyed these commandments ever since his childhood.

He told Jesus, "All these I have kept. What do I still lack?" Although his answer displayed a degree of self-righteousness and superficiality, at the same time he expressed the uneasiness that had driven him to Jesus in the first place. His question, "What do I still lack?" demonstrated a spiritual need that had remained unfulfilled. He needed spiritual guidance to overcome the emptiness in his inner being. He pleaded with Jesus to show him the direction he should take to obtain peace of mind.

Jesus' Reply

Jesus looked at the kneeling young man and loved him. He saw a person who was not far from obtaining salvation. The man lacked one thing, and that was an ability to part with the money that made life enjoyable for him. He kept God's commandments but failed miserably in respect to loving his neighbor as himself. His lifestyle demonstrated selfishness and neglect for the poor. While he lolled in luxury with his abundant possessions, his neighbor felt the daily scourge of grinding poverty.

As the premier counselor in spiritual matters, Jesus instructed the rich young ruler with words that went straight to his heart. Jesus said, "If you wish to be perfect, go and sell all that you have, give the money to the poor, and you will have treasure in heaven; then come follow me."

The young man had to choose whether to keep his material wealth or follow Jesus as his disciple. If he decided to keep his possessions, he would diminish and eventually lose his spirituality. And if he sold his assets and distributed his money, he would lay up treasures in heaven. It was God or money.

With fallen face, the rich young ruler opted for the second and turned away from Jesus. He trusted more in his earthly possessions than in Jesus, who offered him eternal riches.

In reaction, Jesus remarked to his disciples how difficult it is for a rich man to enter the kingdom of heaven. He pointed out that it was easier for a camel to go through the eye of a needle than for a wealthy person to gain entrance into the kingdom of God. Anyone who chooses riches above God has no right to a place in his family.

Application

Do we have to sell our possessions and distribute all our money to the poor? Is the price for attaining perfection so high that we have to live in poverty? Are poor people perfect because they do not own any possessions? Can we accumulate treasures in heaven and still have earthly riches? Do we as Jesus' followers have to live like poverty-stricken people? The answer to all of these questions is no, not necessarily; and yes, because we must love the Lord our God with all our heart, soul, mind, and strength, and love our neighbor as ourselves.

Writing to Timothy, Paul comments on people who have accumulated riches. He says, "Command those who are rich in this present world not to be conceited, nor to put their hope in the uncertainty of wealth, but to put their hope in God, who richly provides us with everything for our enjoyment" (1 Tim. 6:17).

An Adulteress

A Poor Interpretation of the Law

On one occasion, Jesus was in Jerusalem and entered the temple courts for the purpose of teaching the crowd, possibly in the place called Solomon's Colonnade. Here crowds usually gathered to hear religious teachers or government leaders. Jesus sat down to teach the people, and the crowds heard him gladly.

After he had taught the crowd, Jesus noticed that some teachers of the law and Pharisees were coming toward him. They were pushing a woman ahead of them with the clear intention to bring her to Jesus. They wanted Jesus' opinion on a matter pertaining to her.

They placed her in front of him, and closing ranks, they formed a circle with Jesus and the woman in the middle. All of these men were experts in the Law of Moses. One of them served as spokesman, and addressing Jesus, he said, "Teacher, this woman was caught in the act of committing adultery. In the law, Moses commanded us to stone such women. Now what do you say?"

Of course these teachers of the law and Pharisees were correct in pointing to the Law of Moses. But they seemed to have forgotten that not one but two persons engage in an act of adultery. Yet they brought only the woman to Jesus. Did they as men favor the male gender? Did they not know that the law required that both man and woman be executed if she was sexually unfaithful to her (future) husband (Deut. 22:23–24)?

If it was a matter of rape, then only the man had to be executed. Did at least two of the accusers actually observe the man and the woman carrying out the act of adultery? Why did they not warn the man and the woman, to prevent them from committing this sin? The Law of Moses did not stipulate how the guilty should be executed. The penalty of stoning a person to death came from her accusers. Also, executing a person was the prerogative of the Roman governor and not the Jewish leaders.

Two Can Play That Game

By all appearances, the teachers of the law and the Pharisees brought the woman to Jesus for the purpose of setting a trap for him. They slyly asked him what he would say about the accusation and penalty.

If Jesus should answer that the law had lost its force due to its neglect, he would lose his credibility as a teacher of the Scriptures and could be accused of lawlessness. By contrast, if he applied the law and had the woman executed, he would lose face in view of his ministry to forgive sins and restore the sinner. He faced an inescapable dilemma.

The woman's accusers wanted to make Jesus both jury and judge, so that the moral and judicial responsibility would rest on his shoulders. They emphatically asked him, "Now what do *you* say?"

Jesus employed the tactic of delay. Squatting, he started to write something with his finger in the dust on the ground. He could have written words or figures, for what he wrote was unimportant. He stalled for time. But they would not be silenced. They kept on asking Jesus to speak. cmp Jer.

Finally, Jesus straightened himself, stood up, and facing the accusers said, "If anyone is without sin, let him be the first to throw a stone at her." With these words, Jesus referred to the Law of Moses, which said, "The hands of the witnesses must be the first to put [her] to death" (Deut. 17:7).

The men realized that Jesus had used the Scriptures against them. If they had acted hastily in accordance with that law, the woman could have been executed. Then they would be guilty of murder.

Because Jesus referred to the teaching of the law, they were unable to trap him. His stipulation that only a sinless person could cast the first stone caught them off guard. His remark forced them to search their souls.

Once more Jesus used the tactic of silence. He squatted again and wrote something in the dust on the ground. The men kept quiet, for they knew that none was without sin. The younger men waited for the older men to speak. But all of them knew that their consciences condemned them as sinners. At first, the older men quietly slipped away; then those who were younger followed in their footsteps, until no accuser remained.

Jesus' Verdict

When only the woman was left, Jesus stood and asked the woman where her accusers were and whether there was anyone to condemn her. The woman answered that there was no one left. Yet she stood in front of Jesus, who, as the sinless one, had the authority to condemn her. But he also had the authority to forgive sin. He, as the lawgiver, stood above the law, not to annul its force but to alter the verdict. Jesus said, "If no one condemns you, neither do I. Go, and from now on sin no more."

Jesus indicated that she was guilty of the sin of adultery, but by showing mercy, he exonerated her and let her go home. By instructing her to sin no more, he did not imply that she had to be perfect and live a sinless life. He implied that she had to forsake her adulterous life, strive to live a life pleasing to God, and conduct herself as a worthy citizen in his kingdom.

Application

Throughout the Gospel of John, Jesus never asked people to repent. Instead, he showed them their sin, forgave them, and restored them to live in harmony with God's law. He tactfully told the lady in this passage to sin no more.

The air in a room may appear to be dust-free, but when a beam of sunlight illumines the air, it reveals a multitude of floating particles. Though you know you are a sinner, it is not until the Holy Spirit, through the Word of God, enlightens your soul that your sin shows up. When your conscience convicts you, confess your sin to Jesus and he'll forgive you.

A Widow's Offering

Moneychangers at the Temple

During the last week of his earthly life, Jesus spent time at the temple, which he considered to be his Father's house. For him, the temple was a house of prayer for all nations. But moneychangers and merchants of cattle, sheep, and doves had made the area around the temple a den of robbers.

The Jewish people were charged half a shekel per person annually for the temple tax. The temple authorities demanded that the Jews and proselytes who were required to pay this tax do so in the approved Jewish currency. Multitudes of Jews came from nations other than Israel on festival days, and not everyone would have the right currency, so they were forced to turn to moneychangers, who could exchange their money for the correct currency. For their services, the moneychangers charged a price, and a percentage of it went into their own pockets.

Similarly, to accommodate the worshipers who had come from a distance away from Jerusalem, Jewish merchants made available to the public animals for sacrifices. Cattle, sheep, and doves were sold in the temple courts with easy access to the altar of burnt offerings.

While teaching in the temple courts, Jesus had denounced the Pharisees for devouring the houses of widows, and thus he had indicated that the clergy had no concern for the poor.

Afterward Jesus went and took a seat at a place opposite where the worshipers cast their coins into the temple treasury. This was in the Court of the Women, where the temple authorities had placed thirteen chests, all in the form of trumpets. These chests were receptacles for the monetary gifts and offerings donated by the people. Jesus was observing the people casting their coins into these containers. He saw the rich and the poor coming to the receptacles to give their gifts to God.

The Poor Widow's Offering

She was a widow who, when she lost her husband, also lost her source of income. She probably had no sons to support her, and she was too old to marry again. She had often been defrauded by adversaries, and she had no legal defender to protect her. Even though she lived in dire poverty, her hope was in the Lord God, whom she considered to be her protector.

This widow walked into the Court of the Women toward the temple treasury. All she had in her possession were two small coins—the smallest coins in circulation. They amounted to nothing in the eyes of the rich who were ostentatiously throwing into the receptacles large amounts of money. But the widow gave all that she had to God.

Jesus heard the hardly audible tinkling of the two thin copper coins the widow cast into the container. He realized that this was all she had. And even though she could have kept the one for herself and given the other to God, she donated both coins. When her husband was alive, he would at times need money to pay an expense, and his wife would hand him as much as he needed. She knew that before a day had passed, he would reimburse her so that she could purchase necessary food items.

This widow understood that God was her husband and that he would provide for her. When she donated her two copper coins to God, she expected that before the end of the day, he would provide for her in all her needs. Her faith was in her Lord, and she had experienced that God would never forsake her.

Jesus called his disciples to him and said that this poor widow had dropped more into the treasury than all the others. He explained that all the rich gave out of their abundance and perhaps never knew the difference. But this poor soul gave all of her possessions to God. She had nothing left to sustain her life.

God never overlooks the faith his people place in him. He always responds, and that without fail and soon. Although no further details are provided, we can be sure that in tender love and care, God provided richly for her. Here is Jesus' object lesson: it is not the outward quantity of monetary gifts that is significant. Rather, it is the inward quality of a cheerful heart that offers gifts out of gratitude to God.

Application

"The LORD watches over the foreigners; he supports the orphan and the widow, but he thwarts the way of the wicked" (Ps. 146:9). As God's servants and members of the household of faith, we have a moral obligation to care for widows and orphans who are in need of our assistance.

A Teacher of the Law

A Learned Man

Lawyers in Jesus' day were learned scholars who had studied the Scriptures extensively. They had memorized chapters and even whole books and were able to apply the law to everyday life. Due to their many years of learning, they received the respect of the rest of the clergy and the common people in Israel. The New Testament often mentions them together with the Pharisees. These religious leaders fiercely opposed Jesus.

One day a lawyer stood up and addressed Jesus, who had been teaching a crowd of people. The lawyer asked Jesus a question not for the purpose of gaining information but to test him. This schooled lawyer from Jerusalem looked down on Jesus, the prophet from Nazareth. How would this teacher from Galilee answer an expert in the law?

The clergy in Jerusalem were envious of Jesus, who drew large multitudes while they were losing influence. If this lawyer could succeed in humiliating this Galilean teacher, the crowds might

196

turn away from him and go back to the religious instructors and Pharisees.

The lawyer asked, "Teacher, what must I do to inherit eternal life?" He addressed Jesus as teacher—a title of respect. The question he asked was seemingly innocuous but at the same time theologically profound. Inheriting eternal life sounded appealing, but the word *inheriting* implied that someone had to die. Then the last will and testament could be read and the survivors would receive their share of the estate.

The learned man asked Jesus what he had to do to receive the inheritance. Did he have to do something significant that included good works? Apparently without fully understanding the meaning of the term *eternal life*, he had the idea that he would live forever accompanied by heaven's blessings. He wanted to hear from Jesus what he must do to receive these blessings. Yet he knew that God looked at his heart and required that it should be filled with love for God and neighbor.

Jesus answered the lawyer with a counterquestion: "What is written in the law? And how do you read it?" By asking this question, Jesus, not the lawyer, controlled the course of the conversation. Jesus forced him to answer his own question. In a sense, Jesus asked him for a summary of the Ten Commandments.

The lawyer readily responded to these simple questions. He said, "Love the Lord your God with all your heart, with all your soul, with all your strength, and with all your mind, and your neighbor as yourself." He accurately quoted the wording from Deuteronomy 6:5 and Leviticus 19:18. This is the sum and substance of God's law, which can be fulfilled only with love.

Jesus complimented the lawyer: "You have answered correctly. Keep on doing this, and you will live." If the man should do this to the utmost, he would be assured of eternal life. If he considered himself to be a citizen in God's kingdom, he would punctiliously obey the rules and regulations of that kingdom. But if the lawyer should reflect on the thoughts he entertained, the words he spoke, and the deeds he did, he would have to admit that he had not obeyed the summary of the law he had just quoted.

Instead of admitting that he had failed to keep God's law, the lawyer was evasive and asked Jesus to give him a definition of the word *neighbor*. Trying to free himself of any blame, he asked, "Who is my neighbor?" He secretly hoped that Jesus would give him the wrong answer so that he could humiliate Jesus in front of all the people.

The lawyer lived in a circular world; he put himself at the center of the circle. Around him were his immediate relatives, and around them was the extended circle of relatives. The outer circle consisted of all those who were of Jewish descent and those who were converts to Judaism. The lawyer defined the word *neighbor* reciprocally: he is a brother to me and I to him. His interpretation was selfish and limited to his own race. He would love his own people who were within the circle but not those who were strangers and enemies.

The Story in the Form of a Parable

Then Jesus told the lawyer a story that is known as the Parable of the Good Samaritan. He said that a man left Jerusalem and traveled the road to Jericho. But along the way, he was robbed, beaten, and left half-dead.

Soon after the crime was committed, a priest who had completed his temple service in Jerusalem was on his way to his home in Jericho, seventeen miles to the east. The priest glanced at the man lying alongside the road, failed to come near him, and went on.

A Levite similarly went on as he returned home from temple duty. He might have noticed that the priest had not even bothered to stop and help the injured man, so why should the Levite lend a helping hand?

The third person that traveled the Jerusalem-to-Jericho road was a Samaritan merchant. When he saw the wounded man stripped of his clothes and lying in his own blood, he was filled with pity. He helped the man by providing first aid. He gently poured some wine into the wounds as an antiseptic and applied some olive oil as ointment. Then taking some linen from his supply, he tore it into strips and bound up the wounds.

Afterward, the Samaritan placed the man on his donkey, steadied him, and brought him to an inn down the road. There he nursed the wounded man for the rest of the day and throughout the night. The following morning, the Samaritan paid the innkeeper two silver coins and told him to take care of the patient. And should there be extra expense, he told the innkeeper to charge it to his account and he would pay the bill on his next visit.

Jesus related a story filled with revealing overtones:

- First, there was no love lost between a Jew and a Samaritan.
- Next, the priest and the Levite represented the clergy of Israel, who were supposed to help people in need.
- Third, the wounded man could not be identified because, being half-dead, he was unable to speak. Also, his clothes, which marked his identity, had been stolen.
- And last, the story was not about a Jew who found an injured Samaritan along the Jericho road, for that would mark the Jew as a traitor to the Jewish cause.

He did not tell a story about a priest and a Levite who neglected the needs of a wounded Jew. That scenario would seriously damage the relationship between clergy and laity.

Jesus had taught publicly that loving one's neighbor included loving one's enemies. He also had given the people the Golden Rule: "Do to others as you would have them do to you" (Luke 6:31). The lawyer would readily apply this rule to a fellow Jew, but in the story, the stricken man was unidentified, and therefore he did not qualify. Jesus had made his point with the story, and thus he asked the lawyer, "Of the three men, the priest, the Levite, and the Samaritan, which one was a neighbor to the wounded and robbed man?"

The Effect

The lawyer had to answer the question he himself had asked Jesus: "Who is my neighbor?" But he could not make himself to say,

"The Samaritan." Instead, he said that the one who showed mercy was the neighbor.

By telling the story of the Good Samaritan, Jesus focused attention not on the word *neighbor* but on the concept of showing love and compassion to a needy person. Here was a man unable to return anything to the one who helped him. Here was someone who showed mercy and kindness to a fellow human being. Hence, Jesus instructed the lawyer to go and do likewise.

The lesson that Jesus taught was sufficiently powerful to give the lawyer food for thought. If he should bypass a fellow man in need, even if he was of another race, he would transgress the second part of the law's summary: "Love your neighbor as yourself." Then in his neglect, he would undo the effect of the first part of that summary. And by disobeying this summary of the Ten Commandments, he would incur God's wrath.

Application

The scriptural command to love one's neighbor includes reaching out to people of numerous national and ethnic groups. Jesus' call to go and do likewise holds true for us today, just as it did for the lawyer in his day. The Lord asks us to show mercy to all the unfortunate people lying alongside the Jericho road of human life. His is a cry to the affluent to help ease the pain and poverty that countless people experience daily.

Scripture teaches that God's people must be openhanded and generous to the poor in the land, regardless of their ethnicity. The Bible urges Christians to provide financial and social assistance to the poor.

Samaritan Leper

LUKE 17

A Horrible Disease

A Samaritan at the time of Jesus' ministry had contracted leprosy and could no longer be in his own house and community for fear of contaminating others. He was placed in the confines of a leper colony in which both Jews and Samaritans lived together and spent their days until death brought a merciful end to their lives. Racial or religious discriminatory feelings were absent in the leper quarantine because everyone was afflicted with the same disease. These sufferers experienced a gradual destruction of their body parts, including fingers, toes, ears, and nose.

No one of the colony was allowed to come near the village, and villagers stayed away, except for those who provided the necessities of life. Even so, these items were placed at a designated spot where lepers could come and pick them up. The only contact these lepers had with the outside world was when they shouted to those who approached the camp. The leprous Samaritan of Luke 17 lived in this camp with nine other lepers who were Jews.

If it ever happened that the condition of a sufferer improved to the point that he was healed, he was dismissed from the colony. Then he would have to present himself to a priest, who, upon examining him, could declare him healed. Afterward, he was allowed to return to his home, village, or town.

Jesus the Healer

The lepers had heard that Jesus of Nazareth, who had healed countless people, was on his way to Jerusalem to attend one of the religious feasts. They also became aware of his traveling near the leper quarantine. When they saw Jesus and his disciples approaching, they shouted as loud as they could, "Jesus, Master, have mercy on us!" Although the disease progressively destroyed their vocal cords, some of them were still able to make themselves heard. What would Jesus do? Would he approach and touch them? They knew in their hearts that he had the power to perform a miracle merely by speaking the word. And this was exactly what Jesus did.

Jesus said, "Go, show yourselves to the priests." The lepers heard Jesus' command and were astonished. Yet they realized that now they had to act in faith. They had nothing to lose and everything to gain.

The lepers left their camp, and as they started out toward the place where the priests lived, they noticed that where fingers and toes were missing, these now had suddenly appeared. They looked at one another's faces and saw that all of them were healed.

The Samaritan's Gratitude

As the ten healed lepers were walking along toward the priests, one of them stopped in his tracks, turned around, and went toward Jesus. He no longer had to stay away from fellow human beings because the fear of contaminating others had ceased. Regardless of what the other nine lepers wanted to do, he had to rush to Jesus and thank him. In a loud voice, he praised God, and falling at Jesus' feet, he expressed his gratitude from the bottom of his heart. He was the only one who said thank you, and he was a Samaritan. The nine Jews, who should have known better, neglected to show any appreciation to Jesus.

The disappointment was real for Jesus, for he saw that only one out of ten returned to express thanks to him. Although he respected the Samaritan for coming back to him, he was saddened to see the disregard of the nine Jews. Jesus asked three self-evident questions:

1. "Were not all ten cleansed?"
2. "Where then are the other nine?"
3. "Is only a foreigner returning to praise God?"

The nine lepers took for granted the blessing of healing. These nine had received religious education ever since childhood, and yet they neglected to go back to Jesus even when they heard the praises of the Samaritan and saw him return to Jesus. Samaritans had only the first five books of the Old Testament as their Bible, and thus religious instruction for them was insufficient and incomplete. Yet this foreigner, as Jesus called him, had the courtesy to come to him with jubilant praises and thanks.

Jesus then instructed the Samaritan to stand up and go to the priest, for he said, "Your faith has made you well." He healed this person because of his faith, and thus he declared him healed spiritually as well. The nine Jews were healed physically but not spiritually, while the Samaritan, in addition to the gift of a restored body, received the gift of salvation.

Application

The Bible teaches us to give thanks to God for all the blessings he grants us on a daily basis. If we take time to reflect on the countless spiritual and material gifts we receive from God, we may come to a new awareness of our ingratitude.

Though parents train their children to say thank you, at times they are frustrated when their teenagers fail to express gratitude for the parental care and provision they receive.

How many times do we as God's children fail to say thank you to him for daily blessings received? Thus, at mealtime we should thank him for the food that he supplies. Other blessings we should gratefully acknowledge include salvation, forgiveness of sins, eternal life, protecting care, wisdom, faith, love, membership in the family of God, and innumerable financial blessings.

A Crucified Criminal

Three Crosses on a Hill

The cross of Jesus is often pictured between two other crosses. Two criminals were executed at the same time Jesus was put to death.

The Romans would not crucify their own citizens except in cases of treason, but evildoing slaves were crucified as their punishment. To preserve law and order in the Roman provinces, the practice of crucifying slaves also extended to foreigners who had robbed and murdered others. Death by crucifixion was considered the cruelest punishment imaginable and served as a deterrent. There is no information concerning the crimes the two bandits had committed. Yet their conviction was just, according to one of the two criminals nailed to a cross alongside Jesus.

Sometimes the victims were scourged prior to crucifixion. This punishment would open their backs to the bone and sometimes exposed their vital organs. Scourging would cause loss of blood and thus shorten the period of suffering on the cross. Without scourging, victims might hang for more than a day before death ended their misery. In the case of the two criminals, soldiers broke their legs so that asphyxiation hastened their demise.

As a way to humiliate a victim, a judge might order that a board displaying the charge be attached to the cross above the head of the one to be crucified. This happened to Jesus, whose charge read, "Jesus of Nazareth, the king of the Jews." Yet no board indicated the charge of the two common criminals.

A Criminal Acquitted

The crowd and passersby hurled insults not at the two criminals but at Jesus. They taunted him by saying that he who had saved others now should save himself. Others mocked him by calling him king of Israel and telling him to come down from the cross so they could believe in him. Both criminals hanging next to Jesus participated in this mockery. One of them said, "You are the Christ, are you not? Then save yourself and us." But this remark was too much for the other bandit, who severely chided his fellow criminal. He said, "Don't you fear God, since you are under the same sentence of condemnation? We are punished justly, for we are getting what we deserve, but this man has done nothing wrong."

This criminal saw the error of his ways and repented. He knew that his sentence was just and his penalty crucifixion, whereas Jesus was innocent and yet had been given the same sentence. The man had heard Jesus pray to God to forgive his executioners. And he had noticed the love Jesus expressed for his mother and one of his disciples. He probably had heard Jesus teach the multitudes, and perhaps he remembered some of his teachings. When he rebuked his fellow criminal and asked him whether he feared God, he displayed the fear of falling into the hands of the living God.

The man confessed his sin in the presence of the sinless one and said, "Jesus, remember me when you come into your kingdom." He called Jesus by the name the angel had made known to Mary and to Joseph: "for he shall save his people from their sins" (Matt. 1:21). And this Jesus would reign as king on the throne of his father David, whose kingdom would never end.

The criminal understood that Jesus' sovereignty pertained not to an earthly but to a spiritual kingdom. It may be that he had heard John the Baptist and Jesus talk about the kingdom of heaven and had realized that Jesus would be entering heaven. He wanted to be part of this kingdom and therefore pleaded with Jesus to remember him mercifully when he, as king, entered heaven. He desired to be a citizen of that kingdom.

Here was a conversion five minutes before midnight, so to speak. Time was running out for the criminal. Thus he pleaded for grace by asking the king to remember him. He wanted to spend eternity with Jesus and never to be separated from him. On the cross next to Jesus, he asked him not for a place of honor in his kingdom but only to be part of it.

Jesus answered, "I assure you that today you shall be with me in paradise." He did not say that in the future this convert would have a place in his messianic kingdom. Instead, Jesus said that he could be assured that immediately upon death he would be part of that kingdom and receive salvation full and free.

Jesus pardoned the man's sin, accepted him as one of his people, and gave him a place in heaven. Jesus uttered the word *today* to indicate that the man did not have to wait but that immediately upon death he would be with him in paradise. Paradise is another word for heaven; it is a place of perfect harmony and communion with God.

Application

God extends grace to an unrepentant sinner until the moment of death. But when he dies, there is an eternal separation. Therefore, God tells the sinner that now is the time to repent. He says, "Turn to me and live, for why would you die eternally?"

We acknowledge that our sins nailed Jesus to the cross and caused his death. In one of his paintings, Rembrandt van Rijn painted himself among the people who stood around the cross and witnessed the crucifixion. He wanted to indicate that his sins were responsible for Christ's death. Indeed, Jesus died on Calvary's cross for sinners who confess their sins and accept him as their Savior.

PEOPLE WHO
OPPOSED JESUS

JUDAS

A Name of Shame

Fathers and mothers often give their children names taken from the Bible, but parents will avoid calling their son Judas. That name is shunned because of its ignominy.

Yet in the New Testament and other books, Judas is a common name. It comes from the Hebrew word *Judah*, which means "the one who is praised or celebrated." For example, Jesus was born into the tribe of Judah, into which celebrated kings were born; therefore, he was of royal descent and was called king. By contrast, Judas Iscariot, who betrayed Jesus, discredited the name Judah and tarnished its praiseworthiness.

Judas was known as the son of Simon, and by way of identification, he received the name Iscariot. It is possible that the word is a designation of origin, and thus the man is known as Judas of Kerioth. This may have been a town on the southeastern side of the Jordan, and that would mean Judas was a disciple who was not of Galilean descent.

After Jesus spent a whole night in prayer, he had chosen Judas as one of his twelve disciples. In addition to calling Judas his disciple, Jesus had placed him in charge of the money bag and appointed him to be treasurer. He had put his confidence in Judas and given him the responsibility to make the necessary purchases for the daily needs of the disciples and their teacher.

At times, Judas had to care for the poor. But being treasurer proved to be too much of a temptation for him. He was gradually overcome by greed, which led him to steal from the money in the bag.

A Duplicitous Question

Nothing is recorded about Judas Iscariot until the last week of Jesus' earthly life. Six days before the celebration of the Passover Feast, Jesus and the disciples spent the Sabbath in Bethany with Mary, Martha, and Lazarus. In this village, a dinner was given at the house of Simon to honor Jesus and to express gratitude to him for raising Lazarus from the dead. Apparently Jesus was seated near his friend Lazarus, while the hostess Martha was busy serving all the guests.

But Mary had other thoughts. She wanted to honor Jesus in a special way, and she did it by giving him one of the most expensive gifts she owned. She possessed a pint of pure nard, which was an exclusive perfume, an unadulterated product imported from distant regions. The perfume was kept in a long-necked alabaster jar that was white or translucent in color.

Mary came near to Jesus, who was reclining with his feet sticking out away from the table. She broke the neck of the jar and poured the ointment over his feet, and then loosing her hair, she began to dry them with her hair. As can be expected, the whole house was filled with the fragrance of perfume. Loosing her hair and wiping Jesus' feet with it was unbecoming to a lady, but Mary wanted to show her love and devotion to Jesus.

Observing Mary and smelling the perfume, Judas could not constrain himself. He asked, "Why wasn't the perfume sold for three hundred denarii and the money given to the poor?" Three hundred denarii amounted to a whole year's wages for a laborer who worked three hundred days per year.

At face value, Judas's motive could be interpreted as a noble thought, but his fellow disciples had come to know him not as a benefactor of the poor. They knew him as a thief who was interested in lining his own pockets with money from the purse. Instead of reprimanding Judas, Jesus merely told him to leave Mary alone. Then he spoke a word of commendation for Mary and said that she had done a beautiful thing for him. She had kept this perfume for the day of his burial. Expecting Jesus' imminent death, Mary wanted to prepare his body for burial.

Jesus spoke in defense of Mary and thus memorialized her by saying that wherever the gospel would be proclaimed in the world, her deed of kindness would be told. Then he added that there would always be poor people whom his disciples would be able to help at any time they wished, but that they would not always have him in their midst. Jesus told his disciples that Mary was preparing his body for burial, and he indicated that his departure from this earth was at hand.

A Revolting Betrayal

Later, at the celebration of the Passover Feast in the Upper Room, Jesus told the twelve disciples that one of them would betray him. John asked him who that might be. Jesus answered, "It is the one to whom I will give this piece of bread when I have dipped it in the dish." Then dipping the bread in the dish, Jesus gave it to Judas. Jesus used this method to indicate that he was fully aware of Judas's nefarious plan to go to the chief priests and receive thirty pieces of silver as betrayal money.

Jesus gave Judas one last warning, which fell on deaf ears. He said, "Do quickly what you are about to do." But Judas was in the clutches of Satan. He took the bread from Jesus, left the Upper Room, and went outside with a soul as dark as the night.

That same evening, Judas led a band of soldiers and temple guards to the Garden of Gethsemane. Serving as guide, Judas had informed them that there would be twelve men, that is, Jesus and eleven disciples, but that he would kiss Jesus so that the captors could arrest the right man.

Jesus stepped forward to meet his captors and asked, "Whom do you want?" Just at that moment, Judas came up to Jesus, kissed him, and said, "Greetings, Rabbi." Jesus asked him, "Friend, why are you here? Are you betraying the Son of Man with a kiss?" Instead of rebuking him, Jesus addressed him kindly and with two questions revealed to him his sin of betrayal. Even at the time of his arrest, Jesus still ministered kindness to Judas to show him the error of his way.

Judas accompanied the soldiers to the house of Annas, where Jesus was condemned to death because of his admission that he indeed was the Son of God. When Judas became aware of the verdict, he suddenly realized what he had done. He was filled with remorse and hurried from the house of Annas to the temple. With his conscience accusing him, Judas had to get rid of the thirty silver coins burning in his pockets. He went to the chief priests and elders and blurted, "I have sinned by betraying innocent blood."

Judas showed remorse but not repentance. He returned to the chief priests and the elders who had given him the money. Instead, he should have turned repentantly to Jesus to ask him for forgiveness. But by going back to the henchmen, he did the worst thing he could do, for those who are in the service of the devil never grant mercy.

The chief priests and the elders told Judas that his remorse was of no concern to them. It was his problem, not theirs. They did not want to have anything to do with Judas's blood money. So Judas took the thirty coins and threw them into the temple. Although he had removed the coins, he could not remove the burden of guilt from his conscience.

Rejected by the chief priests and the elders, where else could Judas go without Jesus and the disciples? He saw only one way out, and that was to commit suicide. But that was the wrong thing to do, for immediately upon death he would face the Judge of all the earth and would be cast into hell.

Judas went outside the city and hanged himself. There is insufficient information to determine exactly what happened. He might have chosen a tree overhanging the Kidron Valley. The rope could not sustain his body and caused it to drop to the valley floor. Consequently, it was severely mangled and broken in the middle with his insides spilling out. So the life of the traitor Judas came to a tragic end.

Application

There are various downward steps that lead to an ignominious death. The first step is to give in to an enticing temptation by telling oneself that temptation is harmless. The next stage is temptation leading to sin, which results in a guilty conscience. When sin continues to develop, it eventually ends in the final phase, namely, physical and spiritual death.

There are also steps that lead to salvation. The first step is to confirm faith in Jesus Christ; this is followed by listening obediently to his voice and walking steadfastly in his footsteps. This results in enjoying the fullness of life and salvation. Accept Jesus as your personal Savior and live!

Scripture teaches that God does not want anyone to perish. It is his desire that everyone comes to repentance and lives (Ezek. 33:11; 2 Peter 3:9).

PHARISEES

Obeying the Letter of the Law

The Pharisees became known as the "Separated Ones," who looked down on the common people. Because of their haughty attitude, the Pharisees had numerous opponents who did not appreciate their separatist way of life. The Pharisees were the so-called saints who stood above those they considered ceremonially unclean.

In the days of Jesus and the apostles, the number of Pharisees reached about six thousand prominent members. Although there was little love lost between the people of the land and the Pharisees, the masses in Israel followed their leading. They acknowledged the Pharisees as the most accurate interpreters of the law, who were linked to scribes or teachers of the law.

Even though Nicodemus was a Pharisee and became a secret follower of Jesus, the scribes and Pharisees remained adamantly opposed to this teacher from Nazareth. They not only disputed Jesus' teachings; they also criticized his actions, including his healing miracles. But Jesus always based his teaching on the Scriptures and proved the clergy wrong. When they laid a trap for him, he continually overpowered them. Here's a good example.

The Pharisees, with the Herodians (people who supported Roman rule), came to Jesus with the question of whether it was right to pay taxes to Caesar. Thus they placed before him the dilemma of choosing between state and religion. Whichever answer Jesus chose, he would be in trouble.

Jesus rebuked the Pharisees by calling them hypocrites and then asked them to show him the coin for paying the tax to the Roman government. When they complied, he asked them to tell him whose image and inscription were on the coin. They replied, "Caesar's." Then he said to them, "Give to Caesar the things that belong to Caesar, and to God the things that belong to God."

He told them to pay taxes so that they might live in an orderly society, travel along good roads, enjoy a safe environment, and have effective courts of justice. Jesus indicated that they had to honor God with their tithes and offerings and to obey him in harmony with his laws and precepts. Jesus taught that both an earthly kingdom and a spiritual kingdom should exist side by side. He advocated respect for the Roman government, as well as honor for God and his Word.

Later, one of the Pharisees who was an expert in the law wanted to test Jesus and to learn from him which of the commandments was the greatest in the law. This was a hotly debated issue among the learned teachers of the law. As monotheists, who taught the creed of the Hebrews ("Hear, O Israel: The Lord our God, the Lord is one" [Deut. 6:4]), they wanted to know the heart of the Ten Commandments.

Jesus supplied the right answer by giving the Pharisees the summary of the Ten Commandments formulated in Deuteronomy 6:5 and in Leviticus 19:18. He said, "Love the Lord your God with all your heart and with all your soul and with all your mind." He called this the greatest and first commandment. Then he added a second commandment: "Love your neighbor as yourself." He concluded by saying that these two commandments summarize the teachings of the entire Old Testament. Obviously, the expert in the law could not find fault with Jesus' answer.

But Jesus wanted to know what the Pharisees thought about the Christ, so he asked them, "Whose son is he?" He put them on the spot for knowing him to be the Christ but refusing to acknowledge

him as the Messiah. They gave him an evasive answer that was
nevertheless correct: "The son of David." Then Jesus turned to the
Scriptures and asked them why David called the Messiah Lord. He
quoted Psalm 110:1: "The LORD said to my Lord, 'Sit at my right
hand until I put your enemies under your feet.'" And he asked the
Pharisees, "If David calls him Lord, how is he his son?"

The flow of the argument is that the Lord God says to David's
Lord to sit next to him on his throne, and therefore David's Lord is
the Son of God, the Messiah. And yes, indeed, this exalted Messiah,
the son of David, now in the flesh confronted them. The Pharisees
had met their match and were silenced, but they refused to accept
Jesus as the Christ.

Jesus' Scathing Rebuke

Jesus pronounced a series of warnings and woes on the Pharisees and
scribes. He warned his followers not to follow the pernicious example
set by the Jewish leaders. These leaders passed rules on to the people
while they themselves failed to practice what they preached.

The Jewish leaders made a show of their prayer shawls and the
tassels on their garments. They occupied the choice seats in the synagogues, and as they walked through the marketplace, they longed
to be greeted and addressed as Rabbi. Instead of being servants,
they wanted to be served. Instead of being humble, they wanted to
be exalted. Jesus rebuked them for their show of hypocrisy, lack of
sympathy, and spectacle of piety.

Then Jesus pronounced seven woes on the scribes and Pharisees.
In the first, he denounced them for blocking the way to the kingdom of heaven. They themselves did not enter that kingdom, but
at the same time, they hindered others from trying to get into it. By
refusing to acknowledge him as the Christ, they blocked the way
to the kingdom by not permitting others to enter. Jesus addressed
the scribes and Pharisees as hypocrites.

Next, the spiritual leaders in Israel were traveling over land and
across the sea to seek a single new convert. And when they finally
found one, they trained him to become twice as evil as they them-

selves were. Jesus did not have in mind the God-fearing Gentiles who worshiped God in the synagogues. Among these were the Roman centurion Cornelius and Theophilus. Jesus referred specifically to a proselyte who became so heavily influenced by the scribes and Pharisees that they made him doubly worthy to be sent to hell.

The third woe refers to the spiritual blindness of these spiritual leaders, who subverted the truth with frivolous oaths, including swearing by the gold in the temple or by the altar. But oaths are binding and should never be made unless they are kept.

In the fourth woe, Jesus condemned the scribes and Pharisees for meticulously tithing everything, down to the mint and dill in their gardens. But they did so by neglecting the requirements of justice, mercy, and faithfulness.

When Jesus uttered the fifth woe, he called the Pharisees hypocrites and faulted them for cleaning the outside of the cup and dish, while on the inside they were filled with extortion and overindulgence. He noted that they paid careful attention to keeping eating utensils clean so that foods and drink were free from contamination. He instructed them to clean the inside first, namely, their hearts, for then the outside would be clean too.

In the sixth woe, Jesus continued to call the Pharisees hypocrites, for they resembled whitewashed tombs on the outside, but on the inside they were full of human bones and filth. Their religion was nothing more than external appearance, whereas in their hearts they harbored and cultivated the vices of hypocrisy and lawlessness.

And last, Jesus rebuked them once more for being hypocrites who for outward appearance decorated graves and monuments. They boasted about their goodness, but in reality they were descendants of those who killed the prophets that God had sent to them.

Jesus uttered harsh words to the Pharisees by portraying them as snakes. He predicted that they would kill and crucify God's messengers and by implication that they would kill the Son of God by crucifying him. And with an eye to the future, he lamented the coming destruction of Jerusalem and its corrupt leadership.

Nonetheless, some of the Pharisees became Christians in the period between the outpouring of the Holy Spirit on Pentecost in A.D. 30 and the destruction of Jerusalem forty years later. Even the respected Pharisee Gamaliel, a teacher of the law, advised his colleagues in the Sanhedrin to leave the apostles of Jesus alone and to let them go. He recognized that God had ordained the work of the apostles, and he advised the members of the Sanhedrin that they should avoid fighting God.

Application

The word *hypocrite* conjures up ideas of insincerity, duplicity, conceit, and pride. A hypocrite is a pretender who turns goodness into evil, truth into a lie, honesty into deceit, honor into disgrace, and has a complete disregard for God's law.

Hypocrisy is the external performance of an action that lacks any internal commitment. Hypocrites, then, are godless people whose end is both physical and spiritual death. In contrast, honesty and integrity are the hallmarks of Christians who sincerely love both the Lord and their neighbors. They keep God's law not out of compulsion but out of a desire to serve him.

SADDUCEES

Selective Teachings

The Pharisees accepted the entire Old Testament and oral tradition as their guides in life. They therefore had much in common with Jesus and the apostles. But the Sadducees held to only the five books of Moses and did not accord authority to the rest of the Scriptures. They even discarded the traditions of the elders that originated with Moses. They did not hold to the doctrine of a bodily resurrection of the dead but believed that the soul expired with the body. They also rejected the existence of angels and demons, even though cases of demon possession were rampant in Israel during Jesus' ministry.

Jesus encountered the Sadducees only twice, once with the Pharisees and once without them. The first time, they came with the Pharisees and asked for a sign. They had heard about the miracles Jesus had performed by restoring numerous people to health, feeding a multitude, and raising dead people to life. They wanted to know whether he would perform a miracle in their presence and thus demonstrate his supernatural power as a sign from heaven. If he would listen to their request and fail, they could ridicule Jesus and expose him as a fake.

Jesus did not accede to their request, for he perceived their intention. These two parties which were always at odds with each other now came together not to learn from Jesus but to embarrass him. He addressed them by calling attention to signs in nature and history. He said, "When it is evening, you say, 'Fair weather, for the sky is red,' and in the morning, 'Bad weather today, for the sky is red and gloomy.' You know how to interpret correctly the appearance of the sky, but the signs of the times you cannot interpret. An evil and adulterous generation is looking for a sign, but no sign shall be given it except the sign of Jonah."

From everything that they had heard and seen about Jesus, they should have been the first to recognize him as the Messiah. But they refused to accept him as the Christ. And when they failed to read the signs of the times, Jesus directed their attention to the weather and the sign of Jonah. Although the Sadducees disavowed authority to the prophetic books, they knew the historical incident of Jonah's stay in the belly of the fish for three days and three nights. They knew that this prophet had returned to life and in a sense had experienced death and resurrection.

The second time the Sadducees approached Jesus, they came alone because they wanted to test him on the doctrine of the resurrection, which they rejected but the Pharisees taught. They came to him in the last few days of Jesus' earthly life with a fabricated story about a woman who had survived seven husbands, all brothers, and then died. They based this story on the Law of Moses: when a husband dies, his brother should marry the widow (Deut. 25:5–6). The seven husbands died, said the Sadducees, and eventually the woman passed away. "At the resurrection, then," they asked, "whose wife will she be, for all seven were married to her?" They anticipated that Jesus would be stumped; then they could strengthen their denial of the resurrection.

First, Jesus took them to task for refusing to accept the doctrine of the resurrection. He rebuked them for not knowing the Scriptures and the power of God. If they had read the rest of the Old Testament, they would have found passages that teach the resurrection from the dead. They would have admitted that God is powerful indeed. They were on the wrong track by asking him to explain the resurrection. He rebuked them for their rejection of the biblical teaching on this doctrine. He also took them to task for their refusal to accept the doctrine of angels. "In the resurrection they neither marry nor are given in marriage," he said. "They are like the angels in heaven. Concerning the resurrection from the dead, have you not read what God said to you: 'I am the God of Abraham, the God of Isaac, and the God of Jacob'? He is not the God of the dead but of the living."

Instead of scoring a victory, the Sadducees were defeated. The people standing around them heard Jesus' teaching and were astonished.

Application

Among world religions, Christianity stands alone in its teaching of a physical resurrection of the dead. This doctrine is fundamental to the Christian faith. From Pentecost to the present, Christians have faithfully preached the resurrection of the dead. And the universal church confesses the creed, "I believe in the resurrection of the body." That is basic Christianity.

The doctrine of Christ's resurrection is basic to one's faith in him. Everyone who believes that Jesus has been raised physically from the dead is guaranteed eternal life and a physical resurrection of the body in glorified form.

CAIAPHAS

The Trial of Jesus

After Jesus raised Lazarus from the dead, the Sanhedrin met to discuss what action should be taken against Jesus. Caiaphas, as high priest, advised his fellow council members that it would be better if one man died for the people than for the whole Jewish nation to perish. The high priest thought that Jesus' death would be expedient to keep the peace. He wanted to avoid Roman intervention in the event of an insurrection instigated by Jesus and his followers. Without a doubt, the Roman military would slaughter numerous Jews.

In a spiritual sense, the words spoken by Caiaphas were prophetic. Jesus would die not only for the nation of Israel but also for all of God's children. Through his death, Jesus indeed brought together all of God's children and made them one in him.

Caiaphas was a schemer who knew that if Jesus' influence should increase, Caiaphas would lose his high priestly office. To safeguard his position, Caiaphas advised the Sanhedrin to wait for the right moment to remove Jesus. He recommended that the execution not be held during the Passover Feast, when countless Jews would be in Jerusalem. It should be done prior to the festivities. Thus he convened the Sanhedrin in the middle of the night, which was unusual because the gates at the temple area were closed. Hence the trial was held in the palace of the high priest, though for the meeting to have some semblance of legitimacy, it could only be termed an investigation.

During the proceedings, Caiaphas had witnesses appear who testified that Jesus had wanted to break down the temple. But these witnesses' stories did not agree, and their accusation was not sustained.

Then the shrewd high priest decided that he himself should serve as prosecutor. He asked Jesus whether he was the Messiah, the Son of God. When Jesus replied in the affirmative, Caiaphas tore his clothes and accused Jesus of blasphemy.

The Law of Moses stipulated that a person who uttered blasphemy against God ought to be put to death. The members of the Sanhedrin agreed with the high priest that Jesus was worthy of death. Early in the morning, they decided to make the verdict legitimate by handing him over to Governor Pontius Pilate. But when Pilate examined Jesus and repeatedly declared that he found no fault in him, the chief priests shouted, "Crucify him." When Pilate hesitated, they resorted to blackmail. If he should free Jesus, they would inform Caesar that the governor had released a self-proclaimed king. Thus Pilate yielded to their demand and Caiaphas won.

Application

A high priest was God's appointed representative to bring the needs of the people to God in prayer. He had to pray for forgiveness of the sins that the people and he had committed. He had to deal gently with God's people and teach them repentance, as he too had to repent.

Conducting the trial of Jesus, the high priest plotted Jesus' death by crucifixion. He perverted justice, declared the innocent guilty, and forced the governor to execute Jesus. He reasoned that eliminating Jesus was expedient for the nation of Israel. Not Jesus but

Caiaphas was the guilty one who would be tried and condemned in the court of God.

God said, "Be holy, for I am holy" (Lev. 11:44). He holds his people today responsible for the purity of the church. When either leaders or members are falling into grievous sin, he directs the church to exercise discipline. Discipline is designed to have the guilty party repent. If there is no remorse but instead a hardening of the heart, the end result must lead to exclusion from the body.

PILATE

Pilate as Roman Judge

The name Pontius Pilate is forever linked to Jesus of Nazareth. The Apostles' Creed, a confession of faith that is accepted and recited throughout Christendom, features these words: "[Jesus] suffered under Pontius Pilate; was crucified, dead, and buried." Pilate was the Roman governor who sentenced Jesus to die on a cruel cross.

Pilate presumably worked himself up in the ranks of the Roman army and served as a military administrator. From that position, he was recruited to be the governor of Judea. He was given the command of five infantry cohorts and a cavalry regiment that totaled about five thousand military men.

From the Gospels, we know that Pilate was not a fair administrator of Roman justice. Instead of upholding the virtues of honesty and integrity and taking full responsibility as a judge, he succumbed to pressure. He tried to abdicate his juridical duty by asking others to administer justice for him. He sent Jesus to Herod, the ruler of

227

Galilee, who happened to be in Jerusalem for the Passover Feast. He asked the Sanhedrin to pass judgment on Jesus, and he made the crowd choose between Jesus and Barabbas. Pilate compromised to do what was expedient, but at the expense of justice. He sentenced to death a person whom he knew to be innocent.

At daybreak on the Friday morning of the beginning of Passover, the chief priests, with the elders and teachers of the law, took Jesus to Pontius Pilate to have him stand trial. The governor asked them what accusation they brought against Jesus. In reply, they falsely accused him of perverting the nation, refusing to pay taxes to Caesar, and calling himself Christ the king. They also called him a criminal.

Some Jewish authorities were known to have brought to Roman officials religious matters that had nothing to do with Roman law. Pilate was aware of these sly attempts and now saw an excellent opportunity to dismiss the case. He told the Jews to take Jesus and judge him by their own law. But they responded that they lacked the authority to administer capital punishment—a measure that presumably had been taken from them during Pilate's tenure. Pilate, and not the Jewish authorities, held the power of executing criminals.

Roman soldiers brought Jesus inside the palace before Pilate, who asked him, "Are you the king of the Jews?" To Pilate, the charge against Jesus seemed ridiculous, but he had to ask the question. Jesus replied with a counterquestion: "Are you saying this on your own or did others tell you about me?" He could not answer with a brief yes or no, for a yes would have implied that he was a king in a political kingdom. And a negative reply would be a denial of his messianic kingship.

Then Pilate wanted to know what Jesus had done to be brought before him. The chief priests had accused him of being the king of the Jews. Hence the governor expressed his contempt by stating that because he was not a Jew, he was unaware of Jesus' kingship. What would Jesus say to the charges the chief priests had made? If he were not a criminal, then what had he done to deserve this accusation?

Jesus replied, "My kingdom is not of this world. If my kingdom were of this world, my servants would be fighting to keep me from being handed over to the Jews, but now my kingdom is not from here." He admitted that he was a king and that he had servants, but his kingship differed from that of earthly kings. His kingdom was not of this world but had a spiritual origin. He separated himself from the Jewish authorities by indicating that his servants would not keep him from being delivered to the Romans. He insinuated that his kingship was no threat to the Roman government.

The governor wanted to know what kind of kingship Jesus meant. He asked, "So you are a king?" Jesus answered, "You say that I am a king. For this purpose was I born, and for this purpose have I come into the world that I might testify to the truth. Whoever is of the truth listens to my voice." He made it known that he was born a king and that, as such, he had come to testify to the truth. Pilate was unable to understand the meaning of Jesus' words, and he more or less nonchalantly asked, "What is truth?" He did not know that Jesus had taught his disciples that he himself was the truth.

But Pilate had gathered enough evidence to conclude that Jesus was not a criminal and was certainly no threat to Rome. As far as he was concerned, Jesus was innocent, and so he told the Jews, "I do not find any charge against him." If the governor had only kept his word and dismissed the chief priests, he would have spoken justice and set Jesus free.

But as soon as the Jewish leaders heard Pilate's verdict, they told him that Jesus had caused trouble all over Judea, had started it in Galilee, and now had come to Jerusalem. Pilate wanted to know if Jesus was a Galilean. If so, then let Herod Antipas, the ruler of Galilee, take care of the matter.

It so happened that Herod was in Jerusalem that day. Pilate sent Jesus to him, but Herod had no intention of taking on a lawsuit. He had heard about Jesus the miracle-worker, and now he had the opportunity to ask him to perform a miracle in his presence. But Jesus did not even reply to any of his questions. While this was going on, the chief priests and the teachers of the law were leveling charges against Jesus in the presence of Herod. After Herod's soldiers mocked Jesus by dressing him up in an elegant robe, they sent him back to Pilate.

Once more Pilate informed the Jewish authorities that he had found no basis for charges against Jesus, and, he added, neither had Herod. He told them that Jesus was innocent, but to satisfy the accusers, he would scourge him and then set him free. Pilate's sense of justice was distorted, for he was willing to have Jesus suffer the pain of scourging even though he repeatedly declared him guiltless. The governor was a cruel person whose heartlessness was made evident by his causing someone to suffer unjustly.

Once again Pilate faced the predicament of having to deal with an innocent man. Then he remembered his custom of releasing a prisoner at the feast. The crowd would have to choose between two prisoners. They were Jesus, who was innocent, and Barabbas, who was charged with rioting and murder. As the crowd was being given this choice, Pilate's wife sent her husband a warning not to have anything to do with this innocent man. But he ignored her message.

By this time, the chief priests and teachers of the law had incited the crowd to demand the release of Barabbas and not Jesus. When Pilate heard this, he asked what he should do with Jesus, the Christ. They shouted back, "Crucify him." But the governor protested and said that he had not committed a crime. Nonetheless, the crowd kept shouting, "Crucify him." Then once more Pilate backed out of his responsibility to speak justice. He asked for a bowl of water, washed his hands in a symbolic gesture, and indicated that he was innocent of Jesus' blood. He said that his death was the responsibility of the Jewish people.

The Sentencing of Jesus

Inside the palace, Pilate had Jesus scourged. This was a cruel procedure of beating him with a whip of leather thongs that had pieces of metal or bone attached to their ends. The thrashing lacerated Jesus' back, opened major arteries, and may have even affected his vital organs. The soldiers twisted thorn branches into the form of a crown and tortured Jesus by placing it on his head and pressing it down. They mocked him by putting a purple cloth around his shoulders as a semblance of royalty and shouting, "Hail, king of the Jews." Then they slapped him in the face.

Pilate took Jesus outside the palace and made him face the crowd as he was still wearing his crown of thorns and purple cloth. Again the governor told the people that he had not found any charge against him. Wanting to arouse the crowd's pity, he said, "Here's the man!" indicating that Jesus had suffered enough after the scourging and mocking.

The chief priests and the Jewish officials could not be persuaded, for they wanted the death penalty and kept on shouting, "Crucify, crucify!" Pilate again tried to avoid his responsibility by telling the chief priests and their officials to take Jesus and crucify him. He excused himself from responsibility by saying once more that he did not find any charge against Jesus. But the Jewish authorities shouted that Jesus had to die according to their law because he made himself the Son of God.

When Pilate heard the words that Jesus was the Son of God, he was disquieted. He took Jesus inside the palace again and asked him where he was from, but Jesus did not answer him. Pilate then threatened him for being silent: "Don't you know that I have authority to release you and authority to crucify you?" Jesus replied, "You would have no authority over me if it were not given to you from above. Therefore, the one who handed me over to you is guilty of a greater sin." He implied that Pilate was unaware that God had given him authority as a sacred responsibility. And he intimated that the high priest, Caiaphas, who had brought him to Pilate, was the greater sinner because he was familiar with the Scriptures.

Jesus' words upset Pilate so that he tried once again to set him free. But the Jewish leaders knew that the governor was fearful, and thus they took advantage of his apprehension by shouting, "If you release this man, you are no friend of the emperor. Whoever makes himself king opposes the emperor." They threatened the security of Pilate's position as governor, for he feared being deposed by Emperor Tiberius. Pilate would place his personal security above the life of an innocent man. The Jewish authorities used their trump card to defeat Pilate, thereby voting for Emperor Tiberius, who represented Roman occupation of Israel, and against Pilate, their cruel governor.

Pilate, without giving a formal verdict, delivered Jesus to be crucified. And adding insult to injury, he had a sign placed on the cross above Jesus' head that read, "Jesus of Nazareth, King of the Jews."

Application

The Romans prided themselves on having instituted laws that were just and fair. Jesus was tried in a Roman court by a judge who repeatedly declared him not guilty but failed to implement the verdict, sentencing an innocent person to death. It was a travesty of justice!

However, as the bearer of our sins Jesus stood before God's tribunal. "God made him who knew no sin to be sin for us, so that in Christ we might be made right with God" (2 Cor. 5:21). Thus, Jesus took our place to set us free and acquit us in God's presence.

HER☉D ANTIPAS

Herod's Dynasty

Herod Antipas, who reigned during Jesus' lifetime, married the daughter of the Nabatean king, Aretas IV, to promote peace between the Jews and the Arabs. But when decades later Herod Antipas visited his half brother Philip, he fell in love with Philip's wife, Herodias. She agreed to marry Antipas, provided he would divorce his wife, who, upon hearing this news, fled to her father, Aretas. Immediately Herodias, with her daughter Salome, left Philip and moved in with her new husband.

John the Baptist preached a message of repentance and forgiveness at the Jordan and baptized all those who repented of their sins. He publicly rebuked Herod Antipas for marrying Herodias and told him that it was unlawful for him to marry his brother's wife. Both Herod and Herodias were offended, which led to John's arrest when Antipas put him in the Perean prison at Fort Machaerus, which overlooked the eastern shore of the Dead Sea. Herodias waited for an opportunity to kill John, but Herod protected him because he considered John to be a righteous and holy man and liked to listen to him.

Herodias' opportunity came during a birthday party for Antipas. To this celebration he had invited high-ranking officials and military commanders to the palace, which was part of the fort. When the wine was flowing freely, the inebriated Antipas asked Salome to dance for the guests. She was encouraged by her mother and danced lewdly for the guests to please them. Then Antipas said to her, "Ask me anything you want and I'll give it to you, even up to half my kingdom." He emphasized it by swearing oaths. Salome rushed to Herodias and asked her what she should say to her stepfather. Her mother instructed her to ask for the head of John the Baptist on a platter.

Antipas was much upset about this request, for he knew why it was made. His scheming wife wanted to kill the prisoner John. But because of the oaths he had sworn in the presence of his dinner guests, he did not want to disappoint her and ordered an executioner to fulfill Salome's request. Salome took the head and brought it to her mother. And John's disciples came and buried the body.

Herod's Worries

Herod Antipas was a weak man whose thoughtless actions brought him into disrepute with the people. His conscience bothered him, especially when he heard about Jesus' ministry in Galilee and how the people came by the thousands to hear him preach. Also, he had heard about sick people being healed, lepers being cleansed, demons being expelled, and the dead being raised to life. Talk of these miracles was on the lips of everyone in Galilee and Perea.

When Antipas heard the news about the miracle-worker of Galilee, he thought that John the Baptist had come back from the grave, though the Baptist had not performed the miracles Jesus did.

Antipas tried to learn the truth about Jesus. He wanted to know who this person was that performed all these astounding miracles. The more he thought about the matter, the more disturbed he became. Without a doubt, this miracle-worker was righteous and holy, otherwise he would not be able to do these wonders. He longed to meet Jesus, not to believe in him but to observe him perform a miracle in his presence. At the same time, he was disturbed by the threat that the multitudes influenced by Jesus posed to Roman rule.

When Jesus was leaving Galilee to make his last journey to Jerusalem, some Pharisees approached him and warned him to leave the territories of Herod Antipas, who wanted to kill him. Though the Pharisees and Herod were enemies, they had joined forces against Jesus. Jesus told them to be his messengers and deliver this reply to Antipas. He said, "Go tell that fox, 'I am casting out demons and healing people today and tomorrow, and on the third day I will reach my goal.' But I must continue on my way today and tomorrow and the next day, because it would not be right for a prophet to die outside Jerusalem."

Antipas wanted to get rid of Jesus by threatening him so that he would leave Galilee. He did not want to have Jesus' death on his record, for the people had not forgiven him the death of John the Baptist. But Jesus was not at all afraid of Herod. He called him "that fox," which described Antipas's character. Herod was using the Pharisees to get Jesus to go to Jerusalem, where he could be arrested, tried, and executed. The Pharisees were working in collusion with Antipas, who, in Jesus' perception, was behind the scheme.

By way of the Pharisees, Jesus let Herod know that he had nothing to fear of him, because he was helping the people in Herod's territories. And when Jesus spoke about today, tomorrow, and the third day, he referred not to Herod's timetable but to the plan God had determined from eternity.

Antipas had not met Jesus, but that opportunity came when Herod decided to go to Jerusalem for the Passover Feast. While he was there, he unexpectedly received a delegation of chief priests and scribes sent by Governor Pilate with a request to examine and judge Jesus. There was enmity between Herod Antipas and Pontius Pilate, but instead of being annoyed with Pilate's intrusion into his privacy, he saw his opportunity to meet Jesus. Here was his chance to see Jesus perform a miracle.

Herod thought that this prisoner would oblige him to gain for himself an acquittal or a reduced sentence. Herod thought that he had the prisoner in his power, and now he was longing to see a miracle take place. He remembered the time John the Baptist was his prisoner and how John had talked to him and how he had eagerly listened to this prophet. But Jesus treated him with silence. And even though Herod asked him a barrage of questions, Jesus answered not a word.

In the meantime, the chief priests and scribes had raised their voices and in a chorus were vehemently accusing Jesus. They claimed that he had declared himself king of the Jews. Perhaps they were afraid that Antipas would pronounce Jesus innocent and release him, and that would be unacceptable to them. They wanted the death penalty. Even though Herod had no case against Jesus, he was too much of a coward to release him, for he was afraid of the Jewish authorities.

At this time, Herod with his soldiers began to treat Jesus contemptuously, most likely because of his silence and his refusal to perform a miracle. He did not wish to attack Jesus, because his superstition warned him to be careful with this miracle-working preacher from Galilee. Thus he put a gorgeous robe around Jesus' shoulders to signify royalty, mocked him, and sent him back to Pilate. As a consequence of their frustration with Jesus, Herod and Pilate became friends that day, though they had been enemies.

History reveals that a few years later Herod Antipas lost a battle against King Aretas; later, he went to Rome to seek the title of king but was rejected by Emperor Caligula, due to the deceit of a family member of Antipas. Finally, instead of being promoted, he was degraded and sent into exile.

Application

Contrasting Jesus and Herod, we notice striking differences. Jesus is the Lion of Judah and he calls Herod a fox. While Jesus rules as King of Kings, Herod never attained royalty.

By killing John the Baptist and mocking Jesus, Herod incurred God's wrath. He knowingly violated divine commands and eventually paid the penalty. God punished him with loss of face, name, and territory. The well-known adage applies to him: "What you sow you shall also reap."

Conclusion

Throughout his life, Jesus directly and indirectly asked people to follow him. When he saw Peter and his brother, Andrew, casting their net into the Lake of Galilee, he said, "Come, follow me, and I will make you fishers of men." Nicodemus visited him at night, and Jesus sent him as a missionary to the educated ruling class of the Jews in Jerusalem. The Samaritan woman living in the town of Sychar became an ardent evangelist among her own people. And the Gerasene from whom Jesus cast a legion of demons became the first recorded missionary to the Gentiles.

The Great Physician restored the sight of those who were blind, including Bartimaeus of Jericho and the beggar in Jerusalem who was born blind. He healed the crippled woman whom Satan had bound for eighteen years. And he raised from the dead the daughter of Jairus, the young man of Nain, and Lazarus of Bethany. He healed them on the basis of faith and to increase faith in him among the people.

Demonstrations of faith appeared to be equally pronounced among Gentiles and his own people. Jesus stood amazed at the faith of the centurion in Capernaum, who wanted him merely to speak a word of healing because he believed that Jesus had the power to heal from a distance. The persistence of the Syro-Phoenician woman amazed him, for she kept on pleading with him to heal her daughter. But he also admired the faith of the paralytic and his four friends who dug a hole in the flat roof of the house where Jesus taught. The shy woman who suffered from a flow of blood for twelve years demonstrated her faith by touching the hem of his cloak and was healed.

Jesus never dealt harshly with the people who needed help. The adulteress who was brought to Jesus by her accusers heard gentle words from his lips. He told her to go and leave her sinful lifestyle. The rich young man wanted to know how he could gain eternal life. Jesus instructed the man to sell his possessions, to support the poor, and to follow him. He called Mary Magdalene by name in the Garden, and gently taught her that their relationship had entered a new phase now that he had risen from the dead. The twosome on the way to Emmaus received a Scripture lesson from their walking companion, whom they later recognized as their risen Lord.

Jesus rebuked his opponents. Some of them should have been shepherds of the flock but instead were ravenous wolves. They were the Pharisees, known for their hypocrisy; the Sadducees, who neglected and rejected the teaching of Scripture; and the high priest, who misused his sacred calling and protected himself and the nation. Jesus said that Caiaphas had committed a greater sin than the one committed by Pontius Pilate, who did not know the Scriptures.

Even when Jesus confronted Judas in the Upper Room and in the Garden of Gethsemane, he addressed him with gentle words but firmly pointed out the sin of his betrayal. All along, Jesus knew that Judas would betray him, yet his words to him remained kind. Though his disciples knew that Judas pilfered coins from the money bag, Jesus refrained from accusing him.

Jesus profoundly influenced everyone whom he met during his ministry. The closer the people were to the Master, the more they learned. Among them were his disciples, who, after his resurrection, became his apostles to carry the message of salvation to the ends of the earth. And that message continues to spread as it circles the globe, because the gospel of the Lord is unstoppable. Through that gospel, people continue to meet Jesus.

Simon J. Kistemaker was educated at Calvin College, Calvin Theological Seminary, and the Free University of Amsterdam. He was ordained into the ministry of the Christian Reformed Church and served the church in Vernon, British Columbia, Canada.

He has taught at Calvin College, Dordt College, and Reformed Theological Seminary, where he became Professor of New Testament in 1971 and still serves today as professor emeritus.

An internationally recognized lecturer, Kistemaker has written numerous books, including *The Parables*, *The Gospels in Current Study*, and commentaries in the New Testament Commentary series begun by his predecessor, William Hendriksen. Kistemaker contributed commentaries on Acts, 1 Corinthians, 2 Corinthians, Hebrews, the Epistles of James and John, the Epistles of Peter and Jude, and Revelation. Four of these received the Gold Medallion Award from the Evangelical Christian Publishers Association.

He served the Evangelical Theological Society first as president and then as secretary-treasurer for eighteen years.

Unlock the parables of Jesus.

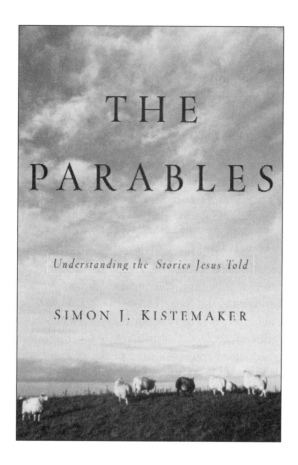

A mong the most-loved stories in Scripture are the parables of Jesus. Taken from real life, the parables conveyed spiritual truth and communicated the message of salvation in simple, everyday language.

In *The Parables*, each parable and parabolic story in the Synoptic Gospels is examined in light of its historical setting and cultural implications, and then applied to the Christian life today.

Highly accessible, informative, and inspiring, *The Parables* is an excellent book for pastors, teachers, students, and all readers who are interested in the significance of the stories Jesus told.